MY MANGA COLLECTION

漫画作品集

THAT TIME I READ SO MUCH
MANGA THAT I NEEDED THIS

》》》 TRACKER 《《《

TO RECORD EVERYTHING,

from the
GOD-TIER VOLUMES *to*
TRASH FAVES *and*
MUST-READS!

VERNIEDA VERGARA
As Featured on
DEN OF GEEK and *BOOK RIOT*

Adams Media
New York   London   Toronto   Sydney   New Delhi

Adams Media
An Imprint of Simon & Schuster, Inc.
100 Technology Center Drive
Stoughton, Massachusetts 02072

First Adams Media trade paperback edition July 2023

ADAMS MEDIA and colophon are trademarks of Simon & Schuster.

For information about special discounts for bulk purchases, please contact Simon & Schuster Special Sales at 1-866-506-1949 or business@simonandschuster.com.

The Simon & Schuster Speakers Bureau can bring authors to your live event. For more information or to book an event, contact the Simon & Schuster Speakers Bureau at 1-866-248-3049 or visit our website at www.simonspeakers.com.

Interior design by Priscilla Yuen
Interior layout by Colleen Cunningham
Interior images © 123RF/hristianin

Manufactured in China

10 9 8 7 6 5 4 3 2 1

ISBN 978-1-5072-2090-0

TABLE OF CONTENTS

INTRODUCTION

Shōnen and dystopian. Shōjo and slice-of-life. Fantasy and sci-fi. And much more!

In manga, there are so many genres and series spanning hundreds of volumes, and every author has something new and exciting to contribute. Maybe you're like me, and your bookshelf is now overflowing with manga volumes; or your phone storage is filled with digital copies; or your librarian knows to reach out to you when the next new volume comes in. Regardless of how you read your manga, or how you keep your manga collection, there has to be a way to keep track of it all...right?

This journal *finally* gives you a way to track the manga you read—whether you buy them from your local bookshop, download them, or borrow them from a friend. Not only can you record the volumes you've read or plan to read, but you can also write down your thoughts about them. Did you love these volumes? Hate them? Do you plan to continue the series until it's complete, or did you lose interest after the third volume?

Beyond the basics, you can use this journal to chronicle your affection for the titular cinnamon roll or defend your stance on why the villain did nothing wrong. You can even note your favorite highlights from a specific manga volume so you can refer to them later. Let's face it: Details start to blur when you're on volume seventeen of a twenty-volume manga.

As you fill this journal with your manga selections and your opinions about them, maybe you'll notice patterns. Do you prefer action-packed fantasy or romantic comedy? Kind, hardworking protagonists or vengeance-seeking antiheroes? Or maybe you love reading every subgenre and want a record of the astonishing variety found in manga. As a manga lover myself, I have put together a reading list of my favorite manga series for you to take a look at and further open your horizons. There's a place for you to rank your top fifty too! (I recommend you write your list in pencil, as your favorite author *may* come out with a new series!) No matter your preferences, let this journal aid your journey through the wonderful and diverse world of manga.

HOW TO USE THIS JOURNAL

This journal contains multiple sections to help you track your manga collection. With each section, there are ways for you to personalize your reactions, ratings, and notes on the manga series you have read.

First, you'll find the customizable table of contents page. Here you can organize the tracker information you will be filling out in the majority of this book. You can look at it to determine where you wrote about *Fullmetal Alchemist* or *Fruits Basket*. Next, you'll move on to the bulk of the journal: the manga series tracker.

The series tracker allows you to log information and thoughts about the manga you're following. Not only does each entry let you record the basics—like title, mangaka, and publisher—you can also indicate whether the manga is currently ongoing or complete and even how many volumes it has. For each volume, you can note what format you read it in and whether it was bought or borrowed. Use the tracker to mark your reading status and rate the series overall, as well as to give ratings for individual volumes. Let's be real: Every series has that one story arc we'd rather pretend didn't exist. You can mark those volumes so you can easily skip those arcs on your next reread of the series.

In the tracker, there's space to jot down your thoughts about each volume. Maybe you want to remember the great fight scenes, or you need to rant about how they killed off your favorite character. Consider these pages a safe space. No judgment here. If you'd rather think about a series as a whole, this journal has you covered. Each manga entry has prompts at the end to help you gather your opinions.

If you're following a long manga, you might be concerned about space. No worries! The tracker is flexible. If you're on a reading binge, you can group multiple volumes into one line in the reading log. If you're tracking each volume separately, there's free space in each manga entry. Feel free to use multiple entries for especially long series!

Need space to keep a running list of manga you plan to buy next? There's a section for that too. And if you don't know what manga to buy, you'll also find a list of fifty must-reads to get you started, as well as a space for you to rank your own top fifty manga series.

Don't feel like you *must* fill out every section for every manga or write a comprehensive to-buy list! It's your journal. Let it serve your needs as it helps you track your (quickly growing) manga collection.

MY MANGA
TABLE OF CONTENTS

Need a space to write an inventory of all of the manga you're tracking? Look no further. This space is for you to keep a written table of contents of your Manga Series Tracker! The first line is filled out for you as an example.

PAGE #	MANGA TITLE	AUTHOR/MANGAKA
X	*Spy x Family*	Tatsuya Endo
10		
16		
22		
28		
34		
40		
46		

PAGE #	MANGA TITLE	AUTHOR/MANGAKA
52		
58		
64		
70		
76		
82		
88		
94		
100		
106		
112		

PAGE #	MANGA TITLE	AUTHOR/MANGAKA
118		
124		
130		
136		
142		
148		
154		
160		
166		
172		
178		

PAGE #	MANGA TITLE	AUTHOR/MANGAKA
184		
190		
196		
202		
208		
214		
220		
226		
232		
238		
244		

📖 MANGA SERIES TRACKER

MANGA TITLE

AUTHOR/MANGAKA

First Volume Publication Date _____   *Final Volume Publication Date* _____

GENRE ○ Shōnen ○ Shōjo ○ Seinen ○ Josei ○ Kodomomuke (Children's)

INTEREST(S)

- ○ Action-Adventure
- ○ Comedy
- ○ Drama
- ○ Dystopian
- ○ Family
- ○ Fantasy
- ○ History
- ○ Horror

- ○ Isekai
- ○ LGBTQ+
- ○ Martial Arts
- ○ Mecha
- ○ Music
- ○ Mystery/Thriller
- ○ Parody
- ○ Romance

- ○ School Life
- ○ Sci-Fi
- ○ Slice-of-Life
- ○ Sports
- ○ Supernatural
- ○ Superpower
- ○ Other: _____

PUBLISHER _____

SERIES STATUS

○ Ongoing ○ Complete ○ Incomplete

TOTAL VOLUMES IN SERIES _____

MY STATUS
- ○ Plan to Read
- ○ Started Reading
- ○ Completed
- ○ Dropped

SERIES RATING

AMAGING
☆ 5
☆
☆
☆
☆ 1
APPALLING

READING LOG

VOLUME **DATE** **RATING** ☆☆☆☆☆

FORMAT ● Physical ● Digital **OWNERSHIP** ● Owned ● Borrowed from: ● Other:
NOTES

VOLUME **DATE** **RATING** ☆☆☆☆☆

FORMAT ● Physical ● Digital **OWNERSHIP** ● Owned ● Borrowed from: ● Other:
NOTES

VOLUME **DATE** **RATING** ☆☆☆☆☆

FORMAT ● Physical ● Digital **OWNERSHIP** ● Owned ● Borrowed from: ● Other:
NOTES

VOLUME **DATE** **RATING** ☆☆☆☆☆

FORMAT ● Physical ● Digital **OWNERSHIP** ● Owned ● Borrowed from: ● Other:
NOTES

VOLUME **DATE** **RATING** ☆☆☆☆☆

FORMAT ● Physical ● Digital **OWNERSHIP** ● Owned ● Borrowed from: ● Other:
NOTES

VOLUME **DATE** **RATING** ☆☆☆☆☆

FORMAT ● Physical ● Digital **OWNERSHIP** ● Owned ● Borrowed from: ● Other:
NOTES

VOLUME DATE RATING ☆☆☆☆☆

FORMAT ◌ Physical ◌ Digital **OWNERSHIP** ◌ Owned ◌ Borrowed from: ◌ Other:

NOTES

VOLUME DATE RATING ☆☆☆☆☆

FORMAT ◌ Physical ◌ Digital **OWNERSHIP** ◌ Owned ◌ Borrowed from: ◌ Other:

NOTES

VOLUME DATE RATING ☆☆☆☆☆

FORMAT ◌ Physical ◌ Digital **OWNERSHIP** ◌ Owned ◌ Borrowed from: ◌ Other:

NOTES

VOLUME DATE RATING ☆☆☆☆☆

FORMAT ◌ Physical ◌ Digital **OWNERSHIP** ◌ Owned ◌ Borrowed from: ◌ Other:

NOTES

VOLUME DATE RATING ☆☆☆☆☆

FORMAT ◌ Physical ◌ Digital **OWNERSHIP** ◌ Owned ◌ Borrowed from: ◌ Other:

NOTES

VOLUME DATE RATING ☆☆☆☆☆

FORMAT ◌ Physical ◌ Digital **OWNERSHIP** ◌ Owned ◌ Borrowed from: ◌ Other:

NOTES

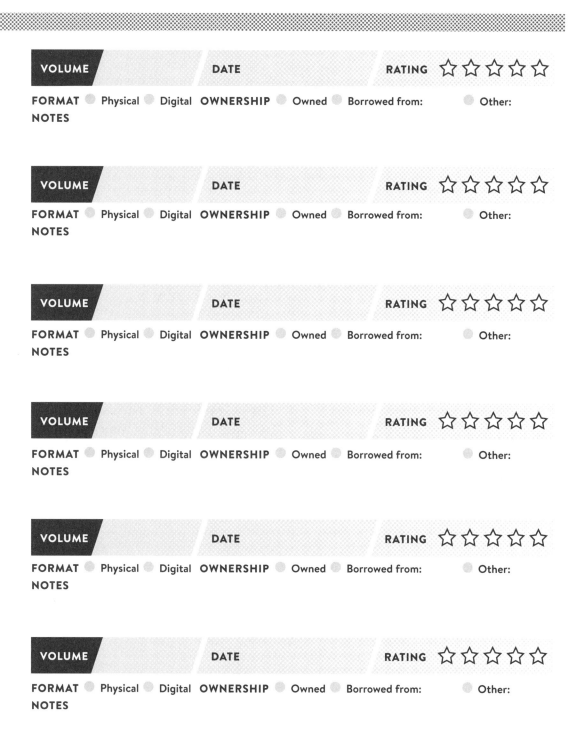

VOLUME **DATE** **RATING** ☆☆☆☆☆

FORMAT ● Physical ● Digital **OWNERSHIP** ● Owned ● Borrowed from: ● Other:

NOTES

VOLUME **DATE** **RATING** ☆☆☆☆☆

FORMAT ● Physical ● Digital **OWNERSHIP** ● Owned ● Borrowed from: ● Other:

NOTES

VOLUME **DATE** **RATING** ☆☆☆☆☆

FORMAT ● Physical ● Digital **OWNERSHIP** ● Owned ● Borrowed from: ● Other:

NOTES

VOLUME **DATE** **RATING** ☆☆☆☆☆

FORMAT ● Physical ● Digital **OWNERSHIP** ● Owned ● Borrowed from: ● Other:

NOTES

VOLUME **DATE** **RATING** ☆☆☆☆☆

FORMAT ● Physical ● Digital **OWNERSHIP** ● Owned ● Borrowed from: ● Other:

NOTES

VOLUME **DATE** **RATING** ☆☆☆☆☆

FORMAT ● Physical ● Digital **OWNERSHIP** ● Owned ● Borrowed from: ● Other:

NOTES

PLOT What hooked you on the plot? What storyline kept/keeps you reading?

What would you have done differently? Where did you want this plot to go?

ART What stood out about the art? How did the art fit the story?

CHARACTERS Who's the most compelling character of the series? The honor of best girl/best boy goes to...

This manga is like (or reminds me of)...

Is there an anime adaptation or film for this manga? If not, do you think there should be one?

Additional notes

📖 MANGA SERIES TRACKER

MANGA TITLE

AUTHOR/MANGAKA

First Volume Publication Date

Final Volume Publication Date

GENRE ○ Shōnen ○ Shōjo ○ Seinen ○ Josei ○ Kodomomuke (Children's)

INTEREST(S)

- ○ Action-Adventure
- ○ Comedy
- ○ Drama
- ○ Dystopian
- ○ Family
- ○ Fantasy
- ○ History
- ○ Horror

- ○ Isekai
- ○ LGBTQ+
- ○ Martial Arts
- ○ Mecha
- ○ Music
- ○ Mystery/Thriller
- ○ Parody
- ○ Romance

- ○ School Life
- ○ Sci-Fi
- ○ Slice-of-Life
- ○ Sports
- ○ Supernatural
- ○ Superpower
- ○ Other:

PUBLISHER

SERIES STATUS

○ Ongoing ○ Complete ○ Incomplete

TOTAL VOLUMES IN SERIES

MY STATUS
- ○ Plan to Read
- ○ Started Reading
- ○ Completed
- ○ Dropped

SERIES RATING

AMAZING

☆ 5
☆
☆
☆
☆ 1

APPALLING

READING LOG

VOLUME   **DATE**   **RATING** ☆☆☆☆☆

FORMAT ○ Physical ○ Digital   **OWNERSHIP** ○ Owned ○ Borrowed from: ○ Other:

NOTES

VOLUME   **DATE**   **RATING** ☆☆☆☆☆

FORMAT ○ Physical ○ Digital   **OWNERSHIP** ○ Owned ○ Borrowed from: ○ Other:

NOTES

VOLUME   **DATE**   **RATING** ☆☆☆☆☆

FORMAT ○ Physical ○ Digital   **OWNERSHIP** ○ Owned ○ Borrowed from: ○ Other:

NOTES

VOLUME   **DATE**   **RATING** ☆☆☆☆☆

FORMAT ○ Physical ○ Digital   **OWNERSHIP** ○ Owned ○ Borrowed from: ○ Other:

NOTES

VOLUME   **DATE**   **RATING** ☆☆☆☆☆

FORMAT ○ Physical ○ Digital   **OWNERSHIP** ○ Owned ○ Borrowed from: ○ Other:

NOTES

VOLUME   **DATE**   **RATING** ☆☆☆☆☆

FORMAT ○ Physical ○ Digital   **OWNERSHIP** ○ Owned ○ Borrowed from: ○ Other:

NOTES

READING LOG

VOLUME **DATE** **RATING** ☆☆☆☆☆

FORMAT ○ Physical ○ Digital **OWNERSHIP** ○ Owned ○ Borrowed from: ○ Other:
NOTES

VOLUME **DATE** **RATING** ☆☆☆☆☆

FORMAT ○ Physical ○ Digital **OWNERSHIP** ○ Owned ○ Borrowed from: ○ Other:
NOTES

VOLUME **DATE** **RATING** ☆☆☆☆☆

FORMAT ○ Physical ○ Digital **OWNERSHIP** ○ Owned ○ Borrowed from: ○ Other:
NOTES

VOLUME **DATE** **RATING** ☆☆☆☆☆

FORMAT ○ Physical ○ Digital **OWNERSHIP** ○ Owned ○ Borrowed from: ○ Other:
NOTES

VOLUME **DATE** **RATING** ☆☆☆☆☆

FORMAT ○ Physical ○ Digital **OWNERSHIP** ○ Owned ○ Borrowed from: ○ Other:
NOTES

VOLUME **DATE** **RATING** ☆☆☆☆☆

FORMAT ○ Physical ○ Digital **OWNERSHIP** ○ Owned ○ Borrowed from: ○ Other:
NOTES

VOLUME **DATE** **RATING** ☆☆☆☆☆

FORMAT ● Physical ● Digital **OWNERSHIP** ● Owned ● Borrowed from: ● Other:

NOTES

VOLUME **DATE** **RATING** ☆☆☆☆☆

FORMAT ● Physical ● Digital **OWNERSHIP** ● Owned ● Borrowed from: ● Other:

NOTES

VOLUME **DATE** **RATING** ☆☆☆☆☆

FORMAT ● Physical ● Digital **OWNERSHIP** ● Owned ● Borrowed from: ● Other:

NOTES

VOLUME **DATE** **RATING** ☆☆☆☆☆

FORMAT ● Physical ● Digital **OWNERSHIP** ● Owned ● Borrowed from: ● Other:

NOTES

VOLUME **DATE** **RATING** ☆☆☆☆☆

FORMAT ● Physical ● Digital **OWNERSHIP** ● Owned ● Borrowed from: ● Other:

NOTES

VOLUME **DATE** **RATING** ☆☆☆☆☆

FORMAT ● Physical ● Digital **OWNERSHIP** ● Owned ● Borrowed from: ● Other:

NOTES

PLOT What hooked you on the plot? What storyline kept/keeps you reading?

What would you have done differently? Where did you want this plot to go?

ART What stood out about the art? How did the art fit the story?

CHARACTERS Who's the most compelling character of the series? The honor of best girl/best boy goes to...

This manga is like (or reminds me of)...

Is there an anime adaptation or film for this manga? If not, do you think there should be one?

Additional notes

📖 MANGA SERIES TRACKER

MANGA TITLE

AUTHOR/MANGAKA

First Volume Publication Date　　　　　*Final Volume Publication Date*

GENRE　　Shōnen　　Shōjo　　Seinen　　Josei　　Kodomomuke (Children's)

INTEREST(S)

- Action-Adventure
- Comedy
- Drama
- Dystopian
- Family
- Fantasy
- History
- Horror

- Isekai
- LGBTQ+
- Martial Arts
- Mecha
- Music
- Mystery/Thriller
- Parody
- Romance

- School Life
- Sci-Fi
- Slice-of-Life
- Sports
- Supernatural
- Superpower
- Other:

PUBLISHER

SERIES STATUS

- Ongoing
- Complete
- Incomplete

TOTAL VOLUMES IN SERIES

MY STATUS
- Plan to Read
- Started Reading
- Completed
- Dropped

SERIES RATING

AMAZING

☆ 5
☆
☆
☆
☆ 1

APPALLING

READING LOG

VOLUME   **DATE**   **RATING** ☆☆☆☆☆

FORMAT ○ Physical ○ Digital   **OWNERSHIP** ○ Owned ○ Borrowed from: ○ Other:

NOTES

VOLUME   **DATE**   **RATING** ☆☆☆☆☆

FORMAT ○ Physical ○ Digital   **OWNERSHIP** ○ Owned ○ Borrowed from: ○ Other:

NOTES

VOLUME   **DATE**   **RATING** ☆☆☆☆☆

FORMAT ○ Physical ○ Digital   **OWNERSHIP** ○ Owned ○ Borrowed from: ○ Other:

NOTES

VOLUME   **DATE**   **RATING** ☆☆☆☆☆

FORMAT ○ Physical ○ Digital   **OWNERSHIP** ○ Owned ○ Borrowed from: ○ Other:

NOTES

VOLUME   **DATE**   **RATING** ☆☆☆☆☆

FORMAT ○ Physical ○ Digital   **OWNERSHIP** ○ Owned ○ Borrowed from: ○ Other:

NOTES

VOLUME   **DATE**   **RATING** ☆☆☆☆☆

FORMAT ○ Physical ○ Digital   **OWNERSHIP** ○ Owned ○ Borrowed from: ○ Other:

NOTES

READING LOG

VOLUME **DATE** **RATING** ☆☆☆☆☆

FORMAT ○ Physical ○ Digital **OWNERSHIP** ○ Owned ○ Borrowed from: ○ Other:

NOTES

VOLUME **DATE** **RATING** ☆☆☆☆☆

FORMAT ○ Physical ○ Digital **OWNERSHIP** ○ Owned ○ Borrowed from: ○ Other:

NOTES

VOLUME **DATE** **RATING** ☆☆☆☆☆

FORMAT ○ Physical ○ Digital **OWNERSHIP** ○ Owned ○ Borrowed from: ○ Other:

NOTES

VOLUME **DATE** **RATING** ☆☆☆☆☆

FORMAT ○ Physical ○ Digital **OWNERSHIP** ○ Owned ○ Borrowed from: ○ Other:

NOTES

VOLUME **DATE** **RATING** ☆☆☆☆☆

FORMAT ○ Physical ○ Digital **OWNERSHIP** ○ Owned ○ Borrowed from: ○ Other:

NOTES

VOLUME **DATE** **RATING** ☆☆☆☆☆

FORMAT ○ Physical ○ Digital **OWNERSHIP** ○ Owned ○ Borrowed from: ○ Other:

NOTES

VOLUME **DATE** **RATING** ☆☆☆☆☆

FORMAT ● Physical ● Digital **OWNERSHIP** ● Owned ● Borrowed from: ● Other:
NOTES

VOLUME **DATE** **RATING** ☆☆☆☆☆

FORMAT ● Physical ● Digital **OWNERSHIP** ● Owned ● Borrowed from: ● Other:
NOTES

VOLUME **DATE** **RATING** ☆☆☆☆☆

FORMAT ● Physical ● Digital **OWNERSHIP** ● Owned ● Borrowed from: ● Other:
NOTES

VOLUME **DATE** **RATING** ☆☆☆☆☆

FORMAT ● Physical ● Digital **OWNERSHIP** ● Owned ● Borrowed from: ● Other:
NOTES

VOLUME **DATE** **RATING** ☆☆☆☆☆

FORMAT ● Physical ● Digital **OWNERSHIP** ● Owned ● Borrowed from: ● Other:
NOTES

VOLUME **DATE** **RATING** ☆☆☆☆☆

FORMAT ● Physical ● Digital **OWNERSHIP** ● Owned ● Borrowed from: ● Other:
NOTES

PLOT What hooked you on the plot? What storyline kept/keeps you reading?

What would you have done differently? Where did you want this plot to go?

ART What stood out about the art? How did the art fit the story?

CHARACTERS Who's the most compelling character of the series? The honor of best girl/best boy goes to...

This manga is like (or reminds me of)...

Is there an anime adaptation or film for this manga? If not, do you think there should be one?

Additional notes

📖 MANGA SERIES TRACKER

MANGA TITLE

AUTHOR/MANGAKA

First Volume Publication Date　　　　　*Final Volume Publication Date*

GENRE　　○ Shōnen　　○ Shōjo　　○ Seinen　　○ Josei　　○ Kodomomuke (Children's)

INTEREST(S)

- Action-Adventure
- Comedy
- Drama
- Dystopian
- Family
- Fantasy
- History
- Horror

- Isekai
- LGBTQ+
- Martial Arts
- Mecha
- Music
- Mystery/Thriller
- Parody
- Romance

- School Life
- Sci-Fi
- Slice-of-Life
- Sports
- Supernatural
- Superpower
- Other:

PUBLISHER

SERIES STATUS

- Ongoing
- Complete
- Incomplete

TOTAL VOLUMES IN SERIES

MY STATUS
- Plan to Read
- Started Reading
- Completed
- Dropped

SERIES RATING

AMAZING

☆ 5
☆
☆
☆
☆ 1

APPALLING

READING LOG

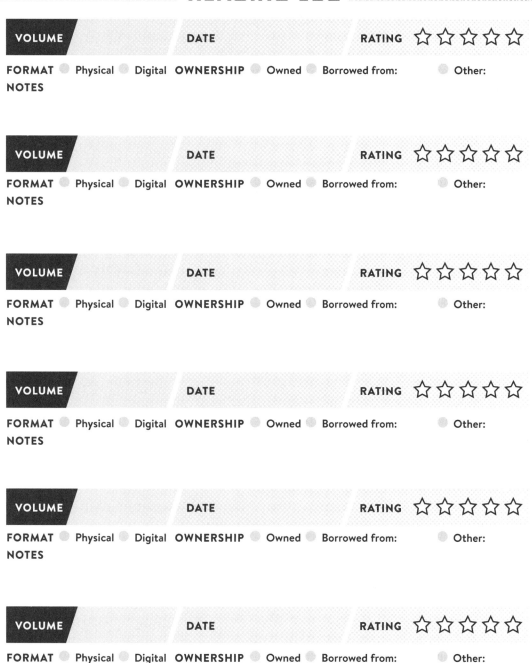

VOLUME **DATE** **RATING** ☆☆☆☆☆

FORMAT ⬤ Physical ⬤ Digital **OWNERSHIP** ⬤ Owned ⬤ Borrowed from: ⬤ Other:

NOTES

VOLUME **DATE** **RATING** ☆☆☆☆☆

FORMAT ⬤ Physical ⬤ Digital **OWNERSHIP** ⬤ Owned ⬤ Borrowed from: ⬤ Other:

NOTES

VOLUME **DATE** **RATING** ☆☆☆☆☆

FORMAT ⬤ Physical ⬤ Digital **OWNERSHIP** ⬤ Owned ⬤ Borrowed from: ⬤ Other:

NOTES

VOLUME **DATE** **RATING** ☆☆☆☆☆

FORMAT ⬤ Physical ⬤ Digital **OWNERSHIP** ⬤ Owned ⬤ Borrowed from: ⬤ Other:

NOTES

VOLUME **DATE** **RATING** ☆☆☆☆☆

FORMAT ⬤ Physical ⬤ Digital **OWNERSHIP** ⬤ Owned ⬤ Borrowed from: ⬤ Other:

NOTES

VOLUME **DATE** **RATING** ☆☆☆☆☆

FORMAT ⬤ Physical ⬤ Digital **OWNERSHIP** ⬤ Owned ⬤ Borrowed from: ⬤ Other:

NOTES

READING LOG

VOLUME | **DATE** | **RATING** ☆☆☆☆☆

FORMAT ● Physical ● Digital **OWNERSHIP** ● Owned ● Borrowed from: ● Other:
NOTES

VOLUME | **DATE** | **RATING** ☆☆☆☆☆

FORMAT ● Physical ● Digital **OWNERSHIP** ● Owned ● Borrowed from: ● Other:
NOTES

VOLUME | **DATE** | **RATING** ☆☆☆☆☆

FORMAT ● Physical ● Digital **OWNERSHIP** ● Owned ● Borrowed from: ● Other:
NOTES

VOLUME | **DATE** | **RATING** ☆☆☆☆☆

FORMAT ● Physical ● Digital **OWNERSHIP** ● Owned ● Borrowed from: ● Other:
NOTES

VOLUME | **DATE** | **RATING** ☆☆☆☆☆

FORMAT ● Physical ● Digital **OWNERSHIP** ● Owned ● Borrowed from: ● Other:
NOTES

VOLUME | **DATE** | **RATING** ☆☆☆☆☆

FORMAT ● Physical ● Digital **OWNERSHIP** ● Owned ● Borrowed from: ● Other:
NOTES

VOLUME **DATE** **RATING** ☆☆☆☆☆

FORMAT ● Physical ● Digital **OWNERSHIP** ● Owned ● Borrowed from: ● Other:

NOTES

VOLUME **DATE** **RATING** ☆☆☆☆☆

FORMAT ● Physical ● Digital **OWNERSHIP** ● Owned ● Borrowed from: ● Other:

NOTES

VOLUME **DATE** **RATING** ☆☆☆☆☆

FORMAT ● Physical ● Digital **OWNERSHIP** ● Owned ● Borrowed from: ● Other:

NOTES

VOLUME **DATE** **RATING** ☆☆☆☆☆

FORMAT ● Physical ● Digital **OWNERSHIP** ● Owned ● Borrowed from: ● Other:

NOTES

VOLUME **DATE** **RATING** ☆☆☆☆☆

FORMAT ● Physical ● Digital **OWNERSHIP** ● Owned ● Borrowed from: ● Other:

NOTES

VOLUME **DATE** **RATING** ☆☆☆☆☆

FORMAT ● Physical ● Digital **OWNERSHIP** ● Owned ● Borrowed from: ● Other:

NOTES

PLOT What hooked you on the plot? What storyline kept/keeps you reading?

What would you have done differently? Where did you want this plot to go?

ART What stood out about the art? How did the art fit the story?

CHARACTERS Who's the most compelling character of the series? The honor of best girl/best boy goes to...

This manga is like (or reminds me of)...

Is there an anime adaptation or film for this manga? If not, do you think there should be one?

Additional notes

MANGA SERIES TRACKER

MANGA TITLE

AUTHOR/MANGAKA

First Volume Publication Date

Final Volume Publication Date

GENRE ○ Shōnen ○ Shōjo ○ Seinen ○ Josei ○ Kodomomuke (Children's)

INTEREST(S)

- ○ Action-Adventure
- ○ Comedy
- ○ Drama
- ○ Dystopian
- ○ Family
- ○ Fantasy
- ○ History
- ○ Horror

- ○ Isekai
- ○ LGBTQ+
- ○ Martial Arts
- ○ Mecha
- ○ Music
- ○ Mystery/Thriller
- ○ Parody
- ○ Romance

- ○ School Life
- ○ Sci-Fi
- ○ Slice-of-Life
- ○ Sports
- ○ Supernatural
- ○ Superpower
- ○ Other:

PUBLISHER

SERIES STATUS
- ○ Ongoing
- ○ Complete
- ○ Incomplete

TOTAL VOLUMES IN SERIES

MY STATUS
- ○ Plan to Read
- ○ Started Reading
- ○ Completed
- ○ Dropped

SERIES RATING

AMAZING

☆ 5
☆
☆
☆
☆ 1

APPALLING

READING LOG

VOLUME   **DATE**   **RATING** ☆☆☆☆☆

FORMAT ○ Physical ○ Digital **OWNERSHIP** ○ Owned ○ Borrowed from: ○ Other:
NOTES

VOLUME   **DATE**   **RATING** ☆☆☆☆☆

FORMAT ○ Physical ○ Digital **OWNERSHIP** ○ Owned ○ Borrowed from: ○ Other:
NOTES

VOLUME   **DATE**   **RATING** ☆☆☆☆☆

FORMAT ○ Physical ○ Digital **OWNERSHIP** ○ Owned ○ Borrowed from: ○ Other:
NOTES

VOLUME   **DATE**   **RATING** ☆☆☆☆☆

FORMAT ○ Physical ○ Digital **OWNERSHIP** ○ Owned ○ Borrowed from: ○ Other:
NOTES

VOLUME   **DATE**   **RATING** ☆☆☆☆☆

FORMAT ○ Physical ○ Digital **OWNERSHIP** ○ Owned ○ Borrowed from: ○ Other:
NOTES

VOLUME   **DATE**   **RATING** ☆☆☆☆☆

FORMAT ○ Physical ○ Digital **OWNERSHIP** ○ Owned ○ Borrowed from: ○ Other:
NOTES

READING LOG

VOLUME   **DATE**   **RATING** ☆☆☆☆☆

FORMAT ○ Physical ○ Digital   **OWNERSHIP** ○ Owned ○ Borrowed from: ○ Other:

NOTES

VOLUME   **DATE**   **RATING** ☆☆☆☆☆

FORMAT ○ Physical ○ Digital   **OWNERSHIP** ○ Owned ○ Borrowed from: ○ Other:

NOTES

VOLUME   **DATE**   **RATING** ☆☆☆☆☆

FORMAT ○ Physical ○ Digital   **OWNERSHIP** ○ Owned ○ Borrowed from: ○ Other:

NOTES

VOLUME   **DATE**   **RATING** ☆☆☆☆☆

FORMAT ○ Physical ○ Digital   **OWNERSHIP** ○ Owned ○ Borrowed from: ○ Other:

NOTES

VOLUME   **DATE**   **RATING** ☆☆☆☆☆

FORMAT ○ Physical ○ Digital   **OWNERSHIP** ○ Owned ○ Borrowed from: ○ Other:

NOTES

VOLUME   **DATE**   **RATING** ☆☆☆☆☆

FORMAT ○ Physical ○ Digital   **OWNERSHIP** ○ Owned ○ Borrowed from: ○ Other:

NOTES

VOLUME   **DATE**   **RATING** ☆ ☆ ☆ ☆ ☆

FORMAT ○ Physical ○ Digital **OWNERSHIP** ○ Owned ○ Borrowed from: ○ Other:
NOTES

VOLUME   **DATE**   **RATING** ☆ ☆ ☆ ☆ ☆

FORMAT ○ Physical ○ Digital **OWNERSHIP** ○ Owned ○ Borrowed from: ○ Other:
NOTES

VOLUME   **DATE**   **RATING** ☆ ☆ ☆ ☆ ☆

FORMAT ○ Physical ○ Digital **OWNERSHIP** ○ Owned ○ Borrowed from: ○ Other:
NOTES

VOLUME   **DATE**   **RATING** ☆ ☆ ☆ ☆ ☆

FORMAT ○ Physical ○ Digital **OWNERSHIP** ○ Owned ○ Borrowed from: ○ Other:
NOTES

VOLUME   **DATE**   **RATING** ☆ ☆ ☆ ☆ ☆

FORMAT ○ Physical ○ Digital **OWNERSHIP** ○ Owned ○ Borrowed from: ○ Other:
NOTES

VOLUME   **DATE**   **RATING** ☆ ☆ ☆ ☆ ☆

FORMAT ○ Physical ○ Digital **OWNERSHIP** ○ Owned ○ Borrowed from: ○ Other:
NOTES

PLOT What hooked you on the plot? What storyline kept/keeps you reading?

What would you have done differently? Where did you want this plot to go?

ART What stood out about the art? How did the art fit the story?

CHARACTERS Who's the most compelling character of the series? The honor of best girl/best boy goes to...

This manga is like (or reminds me of)...

Is there an anime adaptation or film for this manga? If not, do you think there should be one?

Additional notes

📖 MANGA SERIES TRACKER

MANGA TITLE

AUTHOR/MANGAKA

First Volume Publication Date

Final Volume Publication Date

GENRE Shōnen ⬤ Shōjo ⬤ Seinen ⬤ Josei ⬤ Kodomomuke (Children's)

INTEREST(S)

- ⬤ Action-Adventure
- ⬤ Comedy
- ⬤ Drama
- ⬤ Dystopian
- ⬤ Family
- ⬤ Fantasy
- ⬤ History
- ⬤ Horror

- ⬤ Isekai
- ⬤ LGBTQ+
- ⬤ Martial Arts
- ⬤ Mecha
- ⬤ Music
- ⬤ Mystery/Thriller
- ⬤ Parody
- ⬤ Romance

- ⬤ School Life
- ⬤ Sci-Fi
- ⬤ Slice-of-Life
- ⬤ Sports
- ⬤ Supernatural
- ⬤ Superpower
- ⬤ Other:

PUBLISHER

SERIES STATUS
- ⬤ Ongoing
- ⬤ Complete
- ⬤ Incomplete

TOTAL VOLUMES IN SERIES

MY STATUS
- ⬤ Plan to Read
- ⬤ Started Reading
- ⬤ Completed
- ⬤ Dropped

SERIES RATING

AMAZING

☆ 5
☆
☆
☆
☆ 1

APPALLING

READING LOG

VOLUME **DATE** **RATING** ☆☆☆☆☆
FORMAT ○ Physical ○ Digital **OWNERSHIP** ○ Owned ○ Borrowed from: ○ Other:
NOTES

VOLUME **DATE** **RATING** ☆☆☆☆☆
FORMAT ○ Physical ○ Digital **OWNERSHIP** ○ Owned ○ Borrowed from: ○ Other:
NOTES

VOLUME **DATE** **RATING** ☆☆☆☆☆
FORMAT ○ Physical ○ Digital **OWNERSHIP** ○ Owned ○ Borrowed from: ○ Other:
NOTES

VOLUME **DATE** **RATING** ☆☆☆☆☆
FORMAT ○ Physical ○ Digital **OWNERSHIP** ○ Owned ○ Borrowed from: ○ Other:
NOTES

VOLUME **DATE** **RATING** ☆☆☆☆☆
FORMAT ○ Physical ○ Digital **OWNERSHIP** ○ Owned ○ Borrowed from: ○ Other:
NOTES

VOLUME **DATE** **RATING** ☆☆☆☆☆
FORMAT ○ Physical ○ Digital **OWNERSHIP** ○ Owned ○ Borrowed from: ○ Other:
NOTES

READING LOG

VOLUME   **DATE**   **RATING** ☆ ☆ ☆ ☆ ☆

FORMAT ○ Physical ○ Digital   **OWNERSHIP** ○ Owned ○ Borrowed from: ○ Other:

NOTES

VOLUME   **DATE**   **RATING** ☆ ☆ ☆ ☆ ☆

FORMAT ○ Physical ○ Digital   **OWNERSHIP** ○ Owned ○ Borrowed from: ○ Other:

NOTES

VOLUME   **DATE**   **RATING** ☆ ☆ ☆ ☆ ☆

FORMAT ○ Physical ○ Digital   **OWNERSHIP** ○ Owned ○ Borrowed from: ○ Other:

NOTES

VOLUME   **DATE**   **RATING** ☆ ☆ ☆ ☆ ☆

FORMAT ○ Physical ○ Digital   **OWNERSHIP** ○ Owned ○ Borrowed from: ○ Other:

NOTES

VOLUME   **DATE**   **RATING** ☆ ☆ ☆ ☆ ☆

FORMAT ○ Physical ○ Digital   **OWNERSHIP** ○ Owned ○ Borrowed from: ○ Other:

NOTES

VOLUME   **DATE**   **RATING** ☆ ☆ ☆ ☆ ☆

FORMAT ○ Physical ○ Digital   **OWNERSHIP** ○ Owned ○ Borrowed from: ○ Other:

NOTES

VOLUME　　　　**DATE**　　　　**RATING** ☆☆☆☆☆

FORMAT ⚪ Physical ⚪ Digital **OWNERSHIP** ⚪ Owned ⚪ Borrowed from: ⚪ Other:
NOTES

VOLUME　　　　**DATE**　　　　**RATING** ☆☆☆☆☆

FORMAT ⚪ Physical ⚪ Digital **OWNERSHIP** ⚪ Owned ⚪ Borrowed from: ⚪ Other:
NOTES

VOLUME　　　　**DATE**　　　　**RATING** ☆☆☆☆☆

FORMAT ⚪ Physical ⚪ Digital **OWNERSHIP** ⚪ Owned ⚪ Borrowed from: ⚪ Other:
NOTES

VOLUME　　　　**DATE**　　　　**RATING** ☆☆☆☆☆

FORMAT ⚪ Physical ⚪ Digital **OWNERSHIP** ⚪ Owned ⚪ Borrowed from: ⚪ Other:
NOTES

VOLUME　　　　**DATE**　　　　**RATING** ☆☆☆☆☆

FORMAT ⚪ Physical ⚪ Digital **OWNERSHIP** ⚪ Owned ⚪ Borrowed from: ⚪ Other:
NOTES

VOLUME　　　　**DATE**　　　　**RATING** ☆☆☆☆☆

FORMAT ⚪ Physical ⚪ Digital **OWNERSHIP** ⚪ Owned ⚪ Borrowed from: ⚪ Other:
NOTES

PLOT What hooked you on the plot? What storyline kept/keeps you reading?

What would you have done differently? Where did you want this plot to go?

ART What stood out about the art? How did the art fit the story?

CHARACTERS Who's the most compelling character of the series? The honor of best girl/best boy goes to...

This manga is like (or reminds me of)...

Is there an anime adaptation or film for this manga? If not, do you think there should be one?

Additional notes

📖 MANGA SERIES TRACKER

MANGA TITLE

AUTHOR/MANGAKA

First Volume Publication Date   *Final Volume Publication Date*

GENRE   ○ Shōnen   ○ Shōjo   ○ Seinen   ○ Josei   ○ Kodomomuke (Children's)

INTEREST(S)

- ○ Action-Adventure
- ○ Comedy
- ○ Drama
- ○ Dystopian
- ○ Family
- ○ Fantasy
- ○ History
- ○ Horror

- ○ Isekai
- ○ LGBTQ+
- ○ Martial Arts
- ○ Mecha
- ○ Music
- ○ Mystery/Thriller
- ○ Parody
- ○ Romance

- ○ School Life
- ○ Sci-Fi
- ○ Slice-of-Life
- ○ Sports
- ○ Supernatural
- ○ Superpower
- ○ Other:

PUBLISHER

SERIES STATUS

- ○ Ongoing
- ○ Complete
- ○ Incomplete

TOTAL VOLUMES IN SERIES

MY STATUS
- ○ Plan to Read
- ○ Started Reading
- ○ Completed
- ○ Dropped

SERIES RATING

AMAZING
☆ ⑤
☆
☆
☆
☆ ①
APPALLING

READING LOG

VOLUME | **DATE** | **RATING** ☆☆☆☆☆

FORMAT ● Physical ● Digital **OWNERSHIP** ● Owned ● Borrowed from: ● Other:

NOTES

VOLUME | **DATE** | **RATING** ☆☆☆☆☆

FORMAT ● Physical ● Digital **OWNERSHIP** ● Owned ● Borrowed from: ● Other:

NOTES

VOLUME | **DATE** | **RATING** ☆☆☆☆☆

FORMAT ● Physical ● Digital **OWNERSHIP** ● Owned ● Borrowed from: ● Other:

NOTES

VOLUME | **DATE** | **RATING** ☆☆☆☆☆

FORMAT ● Physical ● Digital **OWNERSHIP** ● Owned ● Borrowed from: ● Other:

NOTES

VOLUME | **DATE** | **RATING** ☆☆☆☆☆

FORMAT ● Physical ● Digital **OWNERSHIP** ● Owned ● Borrowed from: ● Other:

NOTES

VOLUME | **DATE** | **RATING** ☆☆☆☆☆

FORMAT ● Physical ● Digital **OWNERSHIP** ● Owned ● Borrowed from: ● Other:

NOTES

READING LOG

VOLUME   **DATE**   **RATING** ☆☆☆☆☆

FORMAT ○ Physical ○ Digital   **OWNERSHIP** ○ Owned ○ Borrowed from: ○ Other:

NOTES

VOLUME   **DATE**   **RATING** ☆☆☆☆☆

FORMAT ○ Physical ○ Digital   **OWNERSHIP** ○ Owned ○ Borrowed from: ○ Other:

NOTES

VOLUME   **DATE**   **RATING** ☆☆☆☆☆

FORMAT ○ Physical ○ Digital   **OWNERSHIP** ○ Owned ○ Borrowed from: ○ Other:

NOTES

VOLUME   **DATE**   **RATING** ☆☆☆☆☆

FORMAT ○ Physical ○ Digital   **OWNERSHIP** ○ Owned ○ Borrowed from: ○ Other:

NOTES

VOLUME   **DATE**   **RATING** ☆☆☆☆☆

FORMAT ○ Physical ○ Digital   **OWNERSHIP** ○ Owned ○ Borrowed from: ○ Other:

NOTES

VOLUME   **DATE**   **RATING** ☆☆☆☆☆

FORMAT ○ Physical ○ Digital   **OWNERSHIP** ○ Owned ○ Borrowed from: ○ Other:

NOTES

VOLUME **DATE** **RATING** ☆☆☆☆☆

FORMAT ● Physical ● Digital **OWNERSHIP** ● Owned ● Borrowed from: ● Other:

NOTES

VOLUME **DATE** **RATING** ☆☆☆☆☆

FORMAT ● Physical ● Digital **OWNERSHIP** ● Owned ● Borrowed from: ● Other:

NOTES

VOLUME **DATE** **RATING** ☆☆☆☆☆

FORMAT ● Physical ● Digital **OWNERSHIP** ● Owned ● Borrowed from: ● Other:

NOTES

VOLUME **DATE** **RATING** ☆☆☆☆☆

FORMAT ● Physical ● Digital **OWNERSHIP** ● Owned ● Borrowed from: ● Other:

NOTES

VOLUME **DATE** **RATING** ☆☆☆☆☆

FORMAT ● Physical ● Digital **OWNERSHIP** ● Owned ● Borrowed from: ● Other:

NOTES

VOLUME **DATE** **RATING** ☆☆☆☆☆

FORMAT ● Physical ● Digital **OWNERSHIP** ● Owned ● Borrowed from: ● Other:

NOTES

PLOT What hooked you on the plot? What storyline kept/keeps you reading?

What would you have done differently? Where did you want this plot to go?

ART What stood out about the art? How did the art fit the story?

CHARACTERS Who's the most compelling character of the series? The honor of best girl/best boy goes to...

This manga is like (or reminds me of)...

Is there an anime adaptation or film for this manga? If not, do you think there should be one?

Additional notes

📖 MANGA SERIES TRACKER

MANGA TITLE

AUTHOR/MANGAKA

First Volume Publication Date _____   *Final Volume Publication Date* _____

GENRE   ○ Shōnen   ○ Shōjo   ○ Seinen   ○ Josei   ○ Kodomomuke (Children's)

INTEREST(S)

- ○ Action-Adventure
- ○ Comedy
- ○ Drama
- ○ Dystopian
- ○ Family
- ○ Fantasy
- ○ History
- ○ Horror

- ○ Isekai
- ○ LGBTQ+
- ○ Martial Arts
- ○ Mecha
- ○ Music
- ○ Mystery/Thriller
- ○ Parody
- ○ Romance

- ○ School Life
- ○ Sci-Fi
- ○ Slice-of-Life
- ○ Sports
- ○ Supernatural
- ○ Superpower
- ○ Other: _____

PUBLISHER _____

SERIES STATUS

○ Ongoing   ○ Complete   ○ Incomplete

TOTAL VOLUMES IN SERIES _____

MY STATUS

- ○ Plan to Read
- ○ Started Reading
- ○ Completed
- ○ Dropped

SERIES RATING

AMATING
☆ 5
☆
☆
☆
☆ 1
APPALLING

READING LOG

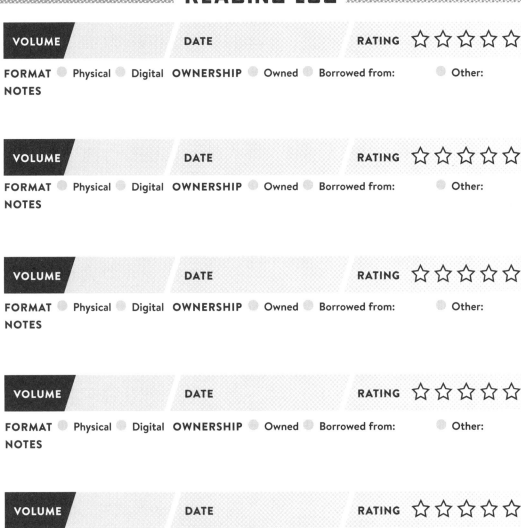

VOLUME **DATE** **RATING** ☆☆☆☆☆

FORMAT ○ Physical ○ Digital **OWNERSHIP** ○ Owned ○ Borrowed from: ○ Other:
NOTES

VOLUME **DATE** **RATING** ☆☆☆☆☆

FORMAT ○ Physical ○ Digital **OWNERSHIP** ○ Owned ○ Borrowed from: ○ Other:
NOTES

VOLUME **DATE** **RATING** ☆☆☆☆☆

FORMAT ○ Physical ○ Digital **OWNERSHIP** ○ Owned ○ Borrowed from: ○ Other:
NOTES

VOLUME **DATE** **RATING** ☆☆☆☆☆

FORMAT ○ Physical ○ Digital **OWNERSHIP** ○ Owned ○ Borrowed from: ○ Other:
NOTES

VOLUME **DATE** **RATING** ☆☆☆☆☆

FORMAT ○ Physical ○ Digital **OWNERSHIP** ○ Owned ○ Borrowed from: ○ Other:
NOTES

VOLUME **DATE** **RATING** ☆☆☆☆☆

FORMAT ○ Physical ○ Digital **OWNERSHIP** ○ Owned ○ Borrowed from: ○ Other:
NOTES

READING LOG

VOLUME   **DATE**   **RATING** ☆☆☆☆☆

FORMAT ● Physical ● Digital   **OWNERSHIP** ● Owned ● Borrowed from: ● Other:

NOTES

VOLUME   **DATE**   **RATING** ☆☆☆☆☆

FORMAT ● Physical ● Digital   **OWNERSHIP** ● Owned ● Borrowed from: ● Other:

NOTES

VOLUME   **DATE**   **RATING** ☆☆☆☆☆

FORMAT ● Physical ● Digital   **OWNERSHIP** ● Owned ● Borrowed from: ● Other:

NOTES

VOLUME   **DATE**   **RATING** ☆☆☆☆☆

FORMAT ● Physical ● Digital   **OWNERSHIP** ● Owned ● Borrowed from: ● Other:

NOTES

VOLUME   **DATE**   **RATING** ☆☆☆☆☆

FORMAT ● Physical ● Digital   **OWNERSHIP** ● Owned ● Borrowed from: ● Other:

NOTES

VOLUME   **DATE**   **RATING** ☆☆☆☆☆

FORMAT ● Physical ● Digital   **OWNERSHIP** ● Owned ● Borrowed from: ● Other:

NOTES

VOLUME　　　　　　　　**DATE**　　　　　　**RATING** ☆☆☆☆☆

FORMAT ● Physical ● Digital **OWNERSHIP** ● Owned ● Borrowed from: ● Other:

NOTES

VOLUME　　　　　　　　**DATE**　　　　　　**RATING** ☆☆☆☆☆

FORMAT ● Physical ● Digital **OWNERSHIP** ● Owned ● Borrowed from: ● Other:

NOTES

VOLUME　　　　　　　　**DATE**　　　　　　**RATING** ☆☆☆☆☆

FORMAT ● Physical ● Digital **OWNERSHIP** ● Owned ● Borrowed from: ● Other:

NOTES

VOLUME　　　　　　　　**DATE**　　　　　　**RATING** ☆☆☆☆☆

FORMAT ● Physical ● Digital **OWNERSHIP** ● Owned ● Borrowed from: ● Other:

NOTES

VOLUME　　　　　　　　**DATE**　　　　　　**RATING** ☆☆☆☆☆

FORMAT ● Physical ● Digital **OWNERSHIP** ● Owned ● Borrowed from: ● Other:

NOTES

VOLUME　　　　　　　　**DATE**　　　　　　**RATING** ☆☆☆☆☆

FORMAT ● Physical ● Digital **OWNERSHIP** ● Owned ● Borrowed from: ● Other:

NOTES

PLOT What hooked you on the plot? What storyline kept/keeps you reading?

What would you have done differently? Where did you want this plot to go?

ART What stood out about the art? How did the art fit the story?

CHARACTERS Who's the most compelling character of the series? The honor of best girl/best boy goes to...

This manga is like (or reminds me of)...

Is there an anime adaptation or film for this manga? If not, do you think there should be one?

Additional notes

MANGA SERIES TRACKER

MANGA TITLE

AUTHOR/MANGAKA

First Volume Publication Date

Final Volume Publication Date

GENRE ◯ Shōnen ◯ Shōjo ◯ Seinen ◯ Josei ◯ Kodomomuke (Children's)

INTEREST(S)

◯ Action-Adventure ◯ Isekai ◯ School Life

◯ Comedy ◯ LGBTQ+ ◯ Sci-Fi

◯ Drama ◯ Martial Arts ◯ Slice-of-Life

◯ Dystopian ◯ Mecha ◯ Sports

◯ Family ◯ Music ◯ Supernatural

◯ Fantasy ◯ Mystery/Thriller ◯ Superpower

◯ History ◯ Parody ◯ Other:

◯ Horror ◯ Romance

PUBLISHER

SERIES STATUS

◯ Ongoing ◯ Complete ◯ Incomplete

TOTAL VOLUMES IN SERIES

MY STATUS ◯ Plan to Read ◯ Completed

◯ Started Reading ◯ Dropped

SERIES RATING

AMAZING

☆ 5
☆
☆
☆
☆ 1

APPALLING

READING LOG

VOLUME   **DATE**   **RATING** ☆☆☆☆☆

FORMAT ○ Physical ○ Digital **OWNERSHIP** ○ Owned ○ Borrowed from: ○ Other:

NOTES

VOLUME   **DATE**   **RATING** ☆☆☆☆☆

FORMAT ○ Physical ○ Digital **OWNERSHIP** ○ Owned ○ Borrowed from: ○ Other:

NOTES

VOLUME   **DATE**   **RATING** ☆☆☆☆☆

FORMAT ○ Physical ○ Digital **OWNERSHIP** ○ Owned ○ Borrowed from: ○ Other:

NOTES

VOLUME   **DATE**   **RATING** ☆☆☆☆☆

FORMAT ○ Physical ○ Digital **OWNERSHIP** ○ Owned ○ Borrowed from: ○ Other:

NOTES

VOLUME   **DATE**   **RATING** ☆☆☆☆☆

FORMAT ○ Physical ○ Digital **OWNERSHIP** ○ Owned ○ Borrowed from: ○ Other:

NOTES

VOLUME   **DATE**   **RATING** ☆☆☆☆☆

FORMAT ○ Physical ○ Digital **OWNERSHIP** ○ Owned ○ Borrowed from: ○ Other:

NOTES

READING LOG

VOLUME   **DATE**   **RATING** ☆☆☆☆☆

FORMAT ○ Physical ○ Digital   **OWNERSHIP** ○ Owned ○ Borrowed from: ○ Other:

NOTES

VOLUME   **DATE**   **RATING** ☆☆☆☆☆

FORMAT ○ Physical ○ Digital   **OWNERSHIP** ○ Owned ○ Borrowed from: ○ Other:

NOTES

VOLUME   **DATE**   **RATING** ☆☆☆☆☆

FORMAT ○ Physical ○ Digital   **OWNERSHIP** ○ Owned ○ Borrowed from: ○ Other:

NOTES

VOLUME   **DATE**   **RATING** ☆☆☆☆☆

FORMAT ○ Physical ○ Digital   **OWNERSHIP** ○ Owned ○ Borrowed from: ○ Other:

NOTES

VOLUME   **DATE**   **RATING** ☆☆☆☆☆

FORMAT ○ Physical ○ Digital   **OWNERSHIP** ○ Owned ○ Borrowed from: ○ Other:

NOTES

VOLUME   **DATE**   **RATING** ☆☆☆☆☆

FORMAT ○ Physical ○ Digital   **OWNERSHIP** ○ Owned ○ Borrowed from: ○ Other:

NOTES

VOLUME **DATE** **RATING** ☆☆☆☆☆

FORMAT ● Physical ● Digital **OWNERSHIP** ● Owned ● Borrowed from: ● Other:
NOTES

VOLUME **DATE** **RATING** ☆☆☆☆☆

FORMAT ● Physical ● Digital **OWNERSHIP** ● Owned ● Borrowed from: ● Other:
NOTES

VOLUME **DATE** **RATING** ☆☆☆☆☆

FORMAT ● Physical ● Digital **OWNERSHIP** ● Owned ● Borrowed from: ● Other:
NOTES

VOLUME **DATE** **RATING** ☆☆☆☆☆

FORMAT ● Physical ● Digital **OWNERSHIP** ● Owned ● Borrowed from: ● Other:
NOTES

VOLUME **DATE** **RATING** ☆☆☆☆☆

FORMAT ● Physical ● Digital **OWNERSHIP** ● Owned ● Borrowed from: ● Other:
NOTES

VOLUME **DATE** **RATING** ☆☆☆☆☆

FORMAT ● Physical ● Digital **OWNERSHIP** ● Owned ● Borrowed from: ● Other:
NOTES

PLOT What hooked you on the plot? What storyline kept/keeps you reading?

What would you have done differently? Where did you want this plot to go?

ART What stood out about the art? How did the art fit the story?

CHARACTERS Who's the most compelling character of the series? The honor of best girl/best boy goes to...

This manga is like (or reminds me of)...

Is there an anime adaptation or film for this manga? If not, do you think there should be one?

Additional notes

MANGA SERIES TRACKER

MANGA TITLE

AUTHOR/MANGAKA

First Volume Publication Date

Final Volume Publication Date

GENRE   ○ Shōnen   ○ Shōjo   ○ Seinen   ○ Josei   ○ Kodomomuke (Children's)

INTEREST(S)

○ Action-Adventure   ○ Isekai   ○ School Life
○ Comedy   ○ LGBTQ+   ○ Sci-Fi
○ Drama   ○ Martial Arts   ○ Slice-of-Life
○ Dystopian   ○ Mecha   ○ Sports
○ Family   ○ Music   ○ Supernatural
○ Fantasy   ○ Mystery/Thriller   ○ Superpower
○ History   ○ Parody   ○ Other:
○ Horror   ○ Romance

PUBLISHER

SERIES STATUS

○ Ongoing   ○ Complete   ○ Incomplete

TOTAL VOLUMES IN SERIES

MY STATUS   ○ Plan to Read   ○ Completed
○ Started Reading   ○ Dropped

SERIES RATING

AMAGING
☆ ⑤

☆

☆

☆

☆ ①
APPALLING

READING LOG

VOLUME **DATE** **RATING** ☆☆☆☆☆

FORMAT ● Physical ● Digital **OWNERSHIP** ● Owned ● Borrowed from: ● Other:

NOTES

VOLUME **DATE** **RATING** ☆☆☆☆☆

FORMAT ● Physical ● Digital **OWNERSHIP** ● Owned ● Borrowed from: ● Other:

NOTES

VOLUME **DATE** **RATING** ☆☆☆☆☆

FORMAT ● Physical ● Digital **OWNERSHIP** ● Owned ● Borrowed from: ● Other:

NOTES

VOLUME **DATE** **RATING** ☆☆☆☆☆

FORMAT ● Physical ● Digital **OWNERSHIP** ● Owned ● Borrowed from: ● Other:

NOTES

VOLUME **DATE** **RATING** ☆☆☆☆☆

FORMAT ● Physical ● Digital **OWNERSHIP** ● Owned ● Borrowed from: ● Other:

NOTES

VOLUME **DATE** **RATING** ☆☆☆☆☆

FORMAT ● Physical ● Digital **OWNERSHIP** ● Owned ● Borrowed from: ● Other:

NOTES

READING LOG

VOLUME | **DATE** | **RATING** ☆☆☆☆☆

FORMAT ○ Physical ○ Digital **OWNERSHIP** ○ Owned ○ Borrowed from: ○ Other:
NOTES

VOLUME | **DATE** | **RATING** ☆☆☆☆☆

FORMAT ○ Physical ○ Digital **OWNERSHIP** ○ Owned ○ Borrowed from: ○ Other:
NOTES

VOLUME | **DATE** | **RATING** ☆☆☆☆☆

FORMAT ○ Physical ○ Digital **OWNERSHIP** ○ Owned ○ Borrowed from: ○ Other:
NOTES

VOLUME | **DATE** | **RATING** ☆☆☆☆☆

FORMAT ○ Physical ○ Digital **OWNERSHIP** ○ Owned ○ Borrowed from: ○ Other:
NOTES

VOLUME | **DATE** | **RATING** ☆☆☆☆☆

FORMAT ○ Physical ○ Digital **OWNERSHIP** ○ Owned ○ Borrowed from: ○ Other:
NOTES

VOLUME | **DATE** | **RATING** ☆☆☆☆☆

FORMAT ○ Physical ○ Digital **OWNERSHIP** ○ Owned ○ Borrowed from: ○ Other:
NOTES

VOLUME   **DATE**   **RATING** ☆☆☆☆☆

FORMAT ● Physical ● Digital **OWNERSHIP** ● Owned ● Borrowed from: ● Other:
NOTES

VOLUME   **DATE**   **RATING** ☆☆☆☆☆

FORMAT ● Physical ● Digital **OWNERSHIP** ● Owned ● Borrowed from: ● Other:
NOTES

VOLUME   **DATE**   **RATING** ☆☆☆☆☆

FORMAT ● Physical ● Digital **OWNERSHIP** ● Owned ● Borrowed from: ● Other:
NOTES

VOLUME   **DATE**   **RATING** ☆☆☆☆☆

FORMAT ● Physical ● Digital **OWNERSHIP** ● Owned ● Borrowed from: ● Other:
NOTES

VOLUME   **DATE**   **RATING** ☆☆☆☆☆

FORMAT ● Physical ● Digital **OWNERSHIP** ● Owned ● Borrowed from: ● Other:
NOTES

VOLUME   **DATE**   **RATING** ☆☆☆☆☆

FORMAT ● Physical ● Digital **OWNERSHIP** ● Owned ● Borrowed from: ● Other:
NOTES

PLOT What hooked you on the plot? What storyline kept/keeps you reading?

What would you have done differently? Where did you want this plot to go?

ART What stood out about the art? How did the art fit the story?

CHARACTERS Who's the most compelling character of the series? The honor of best girl/best boy goes to...

This manga is like (or reminds me of)...

Is there an anime adaptation or film for this manga? If not, do you think there should be one?

Additional notes

MANGA SERIES TRACKER

MANGA TITLE

AUTHOR/MANGAKA

First Volume Publication Date

Final Volume Publication Date

GENRE ○ Shōnen ○ Shōjo ○ Seinen ○ Josei ○ Kodomomuke (Children's)

INTEREST(S)

- Action-Adventure
- Comedy
- Drama
- Dystopian
- Family
- Fantasy
- History
- Horror

- Isekai
- LGBTQ+
- Martial Arts
- Mecha
- Music
- Mystery/Thriller
- Parody
- Romance

- School Life
- Sci-Fi
- Slice-of-Life
- Sports
- Supernatural
- Superpower
- Other:

PUBLISHER

SERIES STATUS
- Ongoing
- Complete
- Incomplete

TOTAL VOLUMES IN SERIES

MY STATUS
- Plan to Read
- Started Reading
- Completed
- Dropped

SERIES RATING

AMAZING

☆ 5
☆
☆
☆
☆ 1

APPALLING

READING LOG

VOLUME   **DATE**   **RATING** ☆☆☆☆☆

FORMAT ○ Physical ○ Digital **OWNERSHIP** ○ Owned ○ Borrowed from: ○ Other:
NOTES

VOLUME   **DATE**   **RATING** ☆☆☆☆☆

FORMAT ○ Physical ○ Digital **OWNERSHIP** ○ Owned ○ Borrowed from: ○ Other:
NOTES

VOLUME   **DATE**   **RATING** ☆☆☆☆☆

FORMAT ○ Physical ○ Digital **OWNERSHIP** ○ Owned ○ Borrowed from: ○ Other:
NOTES

VOLUME   **DATE**   **RATING** ☆☆☆☆☆

FORMAT ○ Physical ○ Digital **OWNERSHIP** ○ Owned ○ Borrowed from: ○ Other:
NOTES

VOLUME   **DATE**   **RATING** ☆☆☆☆☆

FORMAT ○ Physical ○ Digital **OWNERSHIP** ○ Owned ○ Borrowed from: ○ Other:
NOTES

VOLUME   **DATE**   **RATING** ☆☆☆☆☆

FORMAT ○ Physical ○ Digital **OWNERSHIP** ○ Owned ○ Borrowed from: ○ Other:
NOTES

READING LOG

VOLUME   **DATE**   **RATING** ☆☆☆☆☆

FORMAT ○ Physical ○ Digital   **OWNERSHIP** ○ Owned ○ Borrowed from: ○ Other:

NOTES

VOLUME   **DATE**   **RATING** ☆☆☆☆☆

FORMAT ○ Physical ○ Digital   **OWNERSHIP** ○ Owned ○ Borrowed from: ○ Other:

NOTES

VOLUME   **DATE**   **RATING** ☆☆☆☆☆

FORMAT ○ Physical ○ Digital   **OWNERSHIP** ○ Owned ○ Borrowed from: ○ Other:

NOTES

VOLUME   **DATE**   **RATING** ☆☆☆☆☆

FORMAT ○ Physical ○ Digital   **OWNERSHIP** ○ Owned ○ Borrowed from: ○ Other:

NOTES

VOLUME   **DATE**   **RATING** ☆☆☆☆☆

FORMAT ○ Physical ○ Digital   **OWNERSHIP** ○ Owned ○ Borrowed from: ○ Other:

NOTES

VOLUME   **DATE**   **RATING** ☆☆☆☆☆

FORMAT ○ Physical ○ Digital   **OWNERSHIP** ○ Owned ○ Borrowed from: ○ Other:

NOTES

VOLUME **DATE** **RATING** ☆ ☆ ☆ ☆ ☆

FORMAT ○ Physical ○ Digital **OWNERSHIP** ○ Owned ○ Borrowed from: ○ Other:

NOTES

VOLUME **DATE** **RATING** ☆ ☆ ☆ ☆ ☆

FORMAT ○ Physical ○ Digital **OWNERSHIP** ○ Owned ○ Borrowed from: ○ Other:

NOTES

VOLUME **DATE** **RATING** ☆ ☆ ☆ ☆ ☆

FORMAT ○ Physical ○ Digital **OWNERSHIP** ○ Owned ○ Borrowed from: ○ Other:

NOTES

VOLUME **DATE** **RATING** ☆ ☆ ☆ ☆ ☆

FORMAT ○ Physical ○ Digital **OWNERSHIP** ○ Owned ○ Borrowed from: ○ Other:

NOTES

VOLUME **DATE** **RATING** ☆ ☆ ☆ ☆ ☆

FORMAT ○ Physical ○ Digital **OWNERSHIP** ○ Owned ○ Borrowed from: ○ Other:

NOTES

VOLUME **DATE** **RATING** ☆ ☆ ☆ ☆ ☆

FORMAT ○ Physical ○ Digital **OWNERSHIP** ○ Owned ○ Borrowed from: ○ Other:

NOTES

PLOT What hooked you on the plot? What storyline kept/keeps you reading?

What would you have done differently? Where did you want this plot to go?

ART What stood out about the art? How did the art fit the story?

CHARACTERS Who's the most compelling character of the series? The honor of best girl/best boy goes to...

This manga is like (or reminds me of)...

Is there an anime adaptation or film for this manga? If not, do you think there should be one?

Additional notes

📖 MANGA SERIES TRACKER

MANGA TITLE

AUTHOR/MANGAKA

First Volume Publication Date

Final Volume Publication Date

GENRE   ○ Shōnen   ○ Shōjo   ○ Seinen   ○ Josei   ○ Kodomomuke (Children's)

INTEREST(S)

- Action-Adventure
- Comedy
- Drama
- Dystopian
- Family
- Fantasy
- History
- Horror

- Isekai
- LGBTQ+
- Martial Arts
- Mecha
- Music
- Mystery/Thriller
- Parody
- Romance

- School Life
- Sci-Fi
- Slice-of-Life
- Sports
- Supernatural
- Superpower
- Other:

PUBLISHER

SERIES STATUS
- Ongoing
- Complete
- Incomplete

TOTAL VOLUMES IN SERIES

MY STATUS
- Plan to Read
- Started Reading
- Completed
- Dropped

SERIES RATING

AMAZING
☆ 5
☆
☆
☆
☆ 1
APPALLING

READING LOG

VOLUME **DATE** **RATING** ☆☆☆☆☆

FORMAT ⚪ Physical ⚪ Digital **OWNERSHIP** ⚪ Owned ⚪ Borrowed from: ⚪ Other:
NOTES

VOLUME **DATE** **RATING** ☆☆☆☆☆

FORMAT ⚪ Physical ⚪ Digital **OWNERSHIP** ⚪ Owned ⚪ Borrowed from: ⚪ Other:
NOTES

VOLUME **DATE** **RATING** ☆☆☆☆☆

FORMAT ⚪ Physical ⚪ Digital **OWNERSHIP** ⚪ Owned ⚪ Borrowed from: ⚪ Other:
NOTES

VOLUME **DATE** **RATING** ☆☆☆☆☆

FORMAT ⚪ Physical ⚪ Digital **OWNERSHIP** ⚪ Owned ⚪ Borrowed from: ⚪ Other:
NOTES

VOLUME **DATE** **RATING** ☆☆☆☆☆

FORMAT ⚪ Physical ⚪ Digital **OWNERSHIP** ⚪ Owned ⚪ Borrowed from: ⚪ Other:
NOTES

VOLUME **DATE** **RATING** ☆☆☆☆☆

FORMAT ⚪ Physical ⚪ Digital **OWNERSHIP** ⚪ Owned ⚪ Borrowed from: ⚪ Other:
NOTES

READING LOG

VOLUME | **DATE** | **RATING** ☆☆☆☆☆

FORMAT ○ Physical ○ Digital **OWNERSHIP** ○ Owned ○ Borrowed from: ○ Other:

NOTES

VOLUME | **DATE** | **RATING** ☆☆☆☆☆

FORMAT ○ Physical ○ Digital **OWNERSHIP** ○ Owned ○ Borrowed from: ○ Other:

NOTES

VOLUME | **DATE** | **RATING** ☆☆☆☆☆

FORMAT ○ Physical ○ Digital **OWNERSHIP** ○ Owned ○ Borrowed from: ○ Other:

NOTES

VOLUME | **DATE** | **RATING** ☆☆☆☆☆

FORMAT ○ Physical ○ Digital **OWNERSHIP** ○ Owned ○ Borrowed from: ○ Other:

NOTES

VOLUME | **DATE** | **RATING** ☆☆☆☆☆

FORMAT ○ Physical ○ Digital **OWNERSHIP** ○ Owned ○ Borrowed from: ○ Other:

NOTES

VOLUME | **DATE** | **RATING** ☆☆☆☆☆

FORMAT ○ Physical ○ Digital **OWNERSHIP** ○ Owned ○ Borrowed from: ○ Other:

NOTES

VOLUME **DATE** **RATING** ☆☆☆☆☆

FORMAT ● Physical ● Digital **OWNERSHIP** ● Owned ● Borrowed from: ● Other:
NOTES

VOLUME **DATE** **RATING** ☆☆☆☆☆

FORMAT ● Physical ● Digital **OWNERSHIP** ● Owned ● Borrowed from: ● Other:
NOTES

VOLUME **DATE** **RATING** ☆☆☆☆☆

FORMAT ● Physical ● Digital **OWNERSHIP** ● Owned ● Borrowed from: ● Other:
NOTES

VOLUME **DATE** **RATING** ☆☆☆☆☆

FORMAT ● Physical ● Digital **OWNERSHIP** ● Owned ● Borrowed from: ● Other:
NOTES

VOLUME **DATE** **RATING** ☆☆☆☆☆

FORMAT ● Physical ● Digital **OWNERSHIP** ● Owned ● Borrowed from: ● Other:
NOTES

VOLUME **DATE** **RATING** ☆☆☆☆☆

FORMAT ● Physical ● Digital **OWNERSHIP** ● Owned ● Borrowed from: ● Other:
NOTES

MY SERIES NOTES

PLOT What hooked you on the plot? What storyline kept/keeps you reading?

What would you have done differently? Where did you want this plot to go?

ART What stood out about the art? How did the art fit the story?

CHARACTERS Who's the most compelling character of the series? The honor of best girl/best boy goes to...

This manga is like (or reminds me of)...

Is there an anime adaptation or film for this manga? If not, do you think there should be one?

Additional notes

📖 MANGA SERIES TRACKER

MANGA TITLE

AUTHOR/MANGAKA

First Volume Publication Date   *Final Volume Publication Date*

GENRE   ○ Shōnen   ○ Shōjo   ○ Seinen   ○ Josei   ○ Kodomomuke (Children's)

INTEREST(S)

○ Action-Adventure   ○ Isekai   ○ School Life
○ Comedy   ○ LGBTQ+   ○ Sci-Fi
○ Drama   ○ Martial Arts   ○ Slice-of-Life
○ Dystopian   ○ Mecha   ○ Sports
○ Family   ○ Music   ○ Supernatural
○ Fantasy   ○ Mystery/Thriller   ○ Superpower
○ History   ○ Parody   ○ Other:
○ Horror   ○ Romance

PUBLISHER

SERIES STATUS
○ Ongoing   ○ Complete   ○ Incomplete

TOTAL VOLUMES IN SERIES

MY STATUS   ○ Plan to Read   ○ Completed
                ○ Started Reading   ○ Dropped

SERIES RATING

AMAZING
☆ 5
☆
☆
☆
☆ 1
APPALLING

READING LOG

VOLUME   **DATE**   **RATING** ☆☆☆☆☆

FORMAT ● Physical ● Digital **OWNERSHIP** ● Owned ● Borrowed from: ● Other:

NOTES

VOLUME   **DATE**   **RATING** ☆☆☆☆☆

FORMAT ● Physical ● Digital **OWNERSHIP** ● Owned ● Borrowed from: ● Other:

NOTES

VOLUME   **DATE**   **RATING** ☆☆☆☆☆

FORMAT ● Physical ● Digital **OWNERSHIP** ● Owned ● Borrowed from: ● Other:

NOTES

VOLUME   **DATE**   **RATING** ☆☆☆☆☆

FORMAT ● Physical ● Digital **OWNERSHIP** ● Owned ● Borrowed from: ● Other:

NOTES

VOLUME   **DATE**   **RATING** ☆☆☆☆☆

FORMAT ● Physical ● Digital **OWNERSHIP** ● Owned ● Borrowed from: ● Other:

NOTES

VOLUME   **DATE**   **RATING** ☆☆☆☆☆

FORMAT ● Physical ● Digital **OWNERSHIP** ● Owned ● Borrowed from: ● Other:

NOTES

READING LOG

VOLUME **DATE** **RATING** ☆☆☆☆☆

FORMAT ● Physical ● Digital **OWNERSHIP** ● Owned ● Borrowed from: ● Other:
NOTES

VOLUME **DATE** **RATING** ☆☆☆☆☆

FORMAT ● Physical ● Digital **OWNERSHIP** ● Owned ● Borrowed from: ● Other:
NOTES

VOLUME **DATE** **RATING** ☆☆☆☆☆

FORMAT ● Physical ● Digital **OWNERSHIP** ● Owned ● Borrowed from: ● Other:
NOTES

VOLUME **DATE** **RATING** ☆☆☆☆☆

FORMAT ● Physical ● Digital **OWNERSHIP** ● Owned ● Borrowed from: ● Other:
NOTES

VOLUME **DATE** **RATING** ☆☆☆☆☆

FORMAT ● Physical ● Digital **OWNERSHIP** ● Owned ● Borrowed from: ● Other:
NOTES

VOLUME **DATE** **RATING** ☆☆☆☆☆

FORMAT ● Physical ● Digital **OWNERSHIP** ● Owned ● Borrowed from: ● Other:
NOTES

VOLUME　　　　　　　　　　**DATE**　　　　　　　　**RATING** ☆☆☆☆☆

FORMAT ● Physical ● Digital　**OWNERSHIP** ● Owned ● Borrowed from:　　　● Other:

NOTES

VOLUME　　　　　　　　　　**DATE**　　　　　　　　**RATING** ☆☆☆☆☆

FORMAT ● Physical ● Digital　**OWNERSHIP** ● Owned ● Borrowed from:　　　● Other:

NOTES

VOLUME　　　　　　　　　　**DATE**　　　　　　　　**RATING** ☆☆☆☆☆

FORMAT ● Physical ● Digital　**OWNERSHIP** ● Owned ● Borrowed from:　　　● Other:

NOTES

VOLUME　　　　　　　　　　**DATE**　　　　　　　　**RATING** ☆☆☆☆☆

FORMAT ● Physical ● Digital　**OWNERSHIP** ● Owned ● Borrowed from:　　　● Other:

NOTES

VOLUME　　　　　　　　　　**DATE**　　　　　　　　**RATING** ☆☆☆☆☆

FORMAT ● Physical ● Digital　**OWNERSHIP** ● Owned ● Borrowed from:　　　● Other:

NOTES

VOLUME　　　　　　　　　　**DATE**　　　　　　　　**RATING** ☆☆☆☆☆

FORMAT ● Physical ● Digital　**OWNERSHIP** ● Owned ● Borrowed from:　　　● Other:

NOTES

PLOT What hooked you on the plot? What storyline kept/keeps you reading?

What would you have done differently? Where did you want this plot to go?

ART What stood out about the art? How did the art fit the story?

CHARACTERS Who's the most compelling character of the series? The honor of best girl/best boy goes to...

This manga is like (or reminds me of)...

Is there an anime adaptation or film for this manga? If not, do you think there should be one?

Additional notes

MANGA SERIES TRACKER

MANGA TITLE

AUTHOR/MANGAKA

First Volume Publication Date   *Final Volume Publication Date*

GENRE   ○ Shōnen   ○ Shōjo   ○ Seinen   ○ Josei   ○ Kodomomuke (Children's)

INTEREST(S)

○ Action-Adventure   ○ Isekai   ○ School Life
○ Comedy   ○ LGBTQ+   ○ Sci-Fi
○ Drama   ○ Martial Arts   ○ Slice-of-Life
○ Dystopian   ○ Mecha   ○ Sports
○ Family   ○ Music   ○ Supernatural
○ Fantasy   ○ Mystery/Thriller   ○ Superpower
○ History   ○ Parody   ○ Other:
○ Horror   ○ Romance

PUBLISHER

SERIES STATUS

○ Ongoing   ○ Complete   ○ Incomplete

TOTAL VOLUMES IN SERIES

MY STATUS   ○ Plan to Read   ○ Completed
                 ○ Started Reading   ○ Dropped

SERIES RATING

AMAZING
☆ 5
☆
☆
☆
☆ 1
APPALLING

88

READING LOG

VOLUME   **DATE**   **RATING** ☆☆☆☆☆

FORMAT ● Physical ● Digital **OWNERSHIP** ● Owned ● Borrowed from: ● Other:
NOTES

VOLUME   **DATE**   **RATING** ☆☆☆☆☆

FORMAT ● Physical ● Digital **OWNERSHIP** ● Owned ● Borrowed from: ● Other:
NOTES

VOLUME   **DATE**   **RATING** ☆☆☆☆☆

FORMAT ● Physical ● Digital **OWNERSHIP** ● Owned ● Borrowed from: ● Other:
NOTES

VOLUME   **DATE**   **RATING** ☆☆☆☆☆

FORMAT ● Physical ● Digital **OWNERSHIP** ● Owned ● Borrowed from: ● Other:
NOTES

VOLUME   **DATE**   **RATING** ☆☆☆☆☆

FORMAT ● Physical ● Digital **OWNERSHIP** ● Owned ● Borrowed from: ● Other:
NOTES

VOLUME   **DATE**   **RATING** ☆☆☆☆☆

FORMAT ● Physical ● Digital **OWNERSHIP** ● Owned ● Borrowed from: ● Other:
NOTES

READING LOG

VOLUME   DATE   RATING ☆☆☆☆☆

FORMAT ○ Physical ○ Digital **OWNERSHIP** ○ Owned ○ Borrowed from: ○ Other:
NOTES

VOLUME   DATE   RATING ☆☆☆☆☆

FORMAT ○ Physical ○ Digital **OWNERSHIP** ○ Owned ○ Borrowed from: ○ Other:
NOTES

VOLUME   DATE   RATING ☆☆☆☆☆

FORMAT ○ Physical ○ Digital **OWNERSHIP** ○ Owned ○ Borrowed from: ○ Other:
NOTES

VOLUME   DATE   RATING ☆☆☆☆☆

FORMAT ○ Physical ○ Digital **OWNERSHIP** ○ Owned ○ Borrowed from: ○ Other:
NOTES

VOLUME   DATE   RATING ☆☆☆☆☆

FORMAT ○ Physical ○ Digital **OWNERSHIP** ○ Owned ○ Borrowed from: ○ Other:
NOTES

VOLUME   DATE   RATING ☆☆☆☆☆

FORMAT ○ Physical ○ Digital **OWNERSHIP** ○ Owned ○ Borrowed from: ○ Other:
NOTES

VOLUME **DATE** **RATING** ☆☆☆☆☆

FORMAT ● Physical ● Digital **OWNERSHIP** ● Owned ● Borrowed from: ● Other:

NOTES

VOLUME **DATE** **RATING** ☆☆☆☆☆

FORMAT ● Physical ● Digital **OWNERSHIP** ● Owned ● Borrowed from: ● Other:

NOTES

VOLUME **DATE** **RATING** ☆☆☆☆☆

FORMAT ● Physical ● Digital **OWNERSHIP** ● Owned ● Borrowed from: ● Other:

NOTES

VOLUME **DATE** **RATING** ☆☆☆☆☆

FORMAT ● Physical ● Digital **OWNERSHIP** ● Owned ● Borrowed from: ● Other:

NOTES

VOLUME **DATE** **RATING** ☆☆☆☆☆

FORMAT ● Physical ● Digital **OWNERSHIP** ● Owned ● Borrowed from: ● Other:

NOTES

VOLUME **DATE** **RATING** ☆☆☆☆☆

FORMAT ● Physical ● Digital **OWNERSHIP** ● Owned ● Borrowed from: ● Other:

NOTES

PLOT What hooked you on the plot? What storyline kept/keeps you reading?

What would you have done differently? Where did you want this plot to go?

ART What stood out about the art? How did the art fit the story?

CHARACTERS Who's the most compelling character of the series? The honor of best girl/best boy goes to...

This manga is like (or reminds me of)...

Is there an anime adaptation or film for this manga? If not, do you think there should be one?

Additional notes

📖 MANGA SERIES TRACKER

MANGA TITLE

AUTHOR/MANGAKA

First Volume Publication Date

Final Volume Publication Date

GENRE ○ Shōnen ○ Shōjo ○ Seinen ○ Josei ○ Kodomomuke (Children's)

INTEREST(S)

○ Action-Adventure
○ Comedy
○ Drama
○ Dystopian
○ Family
○ Fantasy
○ History
○ Horror

○ Isekai
○ LGBTQ+
○ Martial Arts
○ Mecha
○ Music
○ Mystery/Thriller
○ Parody
○ Romance

○ School Life
○ Sci-Fi
○ Slice-of-Life
○ Sports
○ Supernatural
○ Superpower
○ Other:

PUBLISHER

SERIES STATUS

○ Ongoing ○ Complete ○ Incomplete

TOTAL VOLUMES IN SERIES

MY STATUS
○ Plan to Read ○ Completed
○ Started Reading ○ Dropped

SERIES RATING

AMAGING ☆ 5
☆
☆
☆
☆ 1
APPALLING

READING LOG

VOLUME   **DATE**   **RATING** ☆☆☆☆☆

FORMAT ◯ Physical ◯ Digital   **OWNERSHIP** ◯ Owned ◯ Borrowed from: ◯ Other:

NOTES

VOLUME   **DATE**   **RATING** ☆☆☆☆☆

FORMAT ◯ Physical ◯ Digital   **OWNERSHIP** ◯ Owned ◯ Borrowed from: ◯ Other:

NOTES

VOLUME   **DATE**   **RATING** ☆☆☆☆☆

FORMAT ◯ Physical ◯ Digital   **OWNERSHIP** ◯ Owned ◯ Borrowed from: ◯ Other:

NOTES

VOLUME   **DATE**   **RATING** ☆☆☆☆☆

FORMAT ◯ Physical ◯ Digital   **OWNERSHIP** ◯ Owned ◯ Borrowed from: ◯ Other:

NOTES

VOLUME   **DATE**   **RATING** ☆☆☆☆☆

FORMAT ◯ Physical ◯ Digital   **OWNERSHIP** ◯ Owned ◯ Borrowed from: ◯ Other:

NOTES

VOLUME   **DATE**   **RATING** ☆☆☆☆☆

FORMAT ◯ Physical ◯ Digital   **OWNERSHIP** ◯ Owned ◯ Borrowed from: ◯ Other:

NOTES

READING LOG

VOLUME   **DATE**   **RATING** ☆ ☆ ☆ ☆ ☆

FORMAT ○ Physical ○ Digital   **OWNERSHIP** ○ Owned ○ Borrowed from: ○ Other:

NOTES

VOLUME   **DATE**   **RATING** ☆ ☆ ☆ ☆ ☆

FORMAT ○ Physical ○ Digital   **OWNERSHIP** ○ Owned ○ Borrowed from: ○ Other:

NOTES

VOLUME   **DATE**   **RATING** ☆ ☆ ☆ ☆ ☆

FORMAT ○ Physical ○ Digital   **OWNERSHIP** ○ Owned ○ Borrowed from: ○ Other:

NOTES

VOLUME   **DATE**   **RATING** ☆ ☆ ☆ ☆ ☆

FORMAT ○ Physical ○ Digital   **OWNERSHIP** ○ Owned ○ Borrowed from: ○ Other:

NOTES

VOLUME   **DATE**   **RATING** ☆ ☆ ☆ ☆ ☆

FORMAT ○ Physical ○ Digital   **OWNERSHIP** ○ Owned ○ Borrowed from: ○ Other:

NOTES

VOLUME   **DATE**   **RATING** ☆ ☆ ☆ ☆ ☆

FORMAT ○ Physical ○ Digital   **OWNERSHIP** ○ Owned ○ Borrowed from: ○ Other:

NOTES

VOLUME **DATE** **RATING** ☆☆☆☆☆

FORMAT ○ Physical ○ Digital **OWNERSHIP** ○ Owned ○ Borrowed from: ○ Other:

NOTES

VOLUME **DATE** **RATING** ☆☆☆☆☆

FORMAT ○ Physical ○ Digital **OWNERSHIP** ○ Owned ○ Borrowed from: ○ Other:

NOTES

VOLUME **DATE** **RATING** ☆☆☆☆☆

FORMAT ○ Physical ○ Digital **OWNERSHIP** ○ Owned ○ Borrowed from: ○ Other:

NOTES

VOLUME **DATE** **RATING** ☆☆☆☆☆

FORMAT ○ Physical ○ Digital **OWNERSHIP** ○ Owned ○ Borrowed from: ○ Other:

NOTES

VOLUME **DATE** **RATING** ☆☆☆☆☆

FORMAT ○ Physical ○ Digital **OWNERSHIP** ○ Owned ○ Borrowed from: ○ Other:

NOTES

VOLUME **DATE** **RATING** ☆☆☆☆☆

FORMAT ○ Physical ○ Digital **OWNERSHIP** ○ Owned ○ Borrowed from: ○ Other:

NOTES

PLOT What hooked you on the plot? What storyline kept/keeps you reading?

What would you have done differently? Where did you want this plot to go?

ART What stood out about the art? How did the art fit the story?

CHARACTERS Who's the most compelling character of the series? The honor of best girl/best boy goes to...

This manga is like (or reminds me of)...

Is there an anime adaptation or film for this manga? If not, do you think there should be one?

Additional notes

MANGA SERIES TRACKER

MANGA TITLE

AUTHOR/MANGAKA

First Volume Publication Date

Final Volume Publication Date

GENRE ○ Shōnen   ○ Shōjo   ○ Seinen   ○ Josei   ○ Kodomomuke (Children's)

INTEREST(S)

- ○ Action-Adventure
- ○ Comedy
- ○ Drama
- ○ Dystopian
- ○ Family
- ○ Fantasy
- ○ History
- ○ Horror

- ○ Isekai
- ○ LGBTQ+
- ○ Martial Arts
- ○ Mecha
- ○ Music
- ○ Mystery/Thriller
- ○ Parody
- ○ Romance

- ○ School Life
- ○ Sci-Fi
- ○ Slice-of-Life
- ○ Sports
- ○ Supernatural
- ○ Superpower
- ○ Other:

PUBLISHER

SERIES STATUS

- ○ Ongoing
- ○ Complete
- ○ Incomplete

TOTAL VOLUMES IN SERIES

MY STATUS
- ○ Plan to Read
- ○ Started Reading
- ○ Completed
- ○ Dropped

SERIES RATING

AMAZING
☆ 5
☆
☆
☆
☆ 1
APPALLING

READING LOG

VOLUME **DATE** **RATING** ☆☆☆☆☆

FORMAT ○ Physical ○ Digital **OWNERSHIP** ○ Owned ○ Borrowed from: ○ Other:

NOTES

VOLUME **DATE** **RATING** ☆☆☆☆☆

FORMAT ○ Physical ○ Digital **OWNERSHIP** ○ Owned ○ Borrowed from: ○ Other:

NOTES

VOLUME **DATE** **RATING** ☆☆☆☆☆

FORMAT ○ Physical ○ Digital **OWNERSHIP** ○ Owned ○ Borrowed from: ○ Other:

NOTES

VOLUME **DATE** **RATING** ☆☆☆☆☆

FORMAT ○ Physical ○ Digital **OWNERSHIP** ○ Owned ○ Borrowed from: ○ Other:

NOTES

VOLUME **DATE** **RATING** ☆☆☆☆☆

FORMAT ○ Physical ○ Digital **OWNERSHIP** ○ Owned ○ Borrowed from: ○ Other:

NOTES

VOLUME **DATE** **RATING** ☆☆☆☆☆

FORMAT ○ Physical ○ Digital **OWNERSHIP** ○ Owned ○ Borrowed from: ○ Other:

NOTES

READING LOG

VOLUME   **DATE**   **RATING** ☆☆☆☆☆

FORMAT ○ Physical ○ Digital   **OWNERSHIP** ○ Owned ○ Borrowed from: ○ Other:

NOTES

VOLUME   **DATE**   **RATING** ☆☆☆☆☆

FORMAT ○ Physical ○ Digital   **OWNERSHIP** ○ Owned ○ Borrowed from: ○ Other:

NOTES

VOLUME   **DATE**   **RATING** ☆☆☆☆☆

FORMAT ○ Physical ○ Digital   **OWNERSHIP** ○ Owned ○ Borrowed from: ○ Other:

NOTES

VOLUME   **DATE**   **RATING** ☆☆☆☆☆

FORMAT ○ Physical ○ Digital   **OWNERSHIP** ○ Owned ○ Borrowed from: ○ Other:

NOTES

VOLUME   **DATE**   **RATING** ☆☆☆☆☆

FORMAT ○ Physical ○ Digital   **OWNERSHIP** ○ Owned ○ Borrowed from: ○ Other:

NOTES

VOLUME   **DATE**   **RATING** ☆☆☆☆☆

FORMAT ○ Physical ○ Digital   **OWNERSHIP** ○ Owned ○ Borrowed from: ○ Other:

NOTES

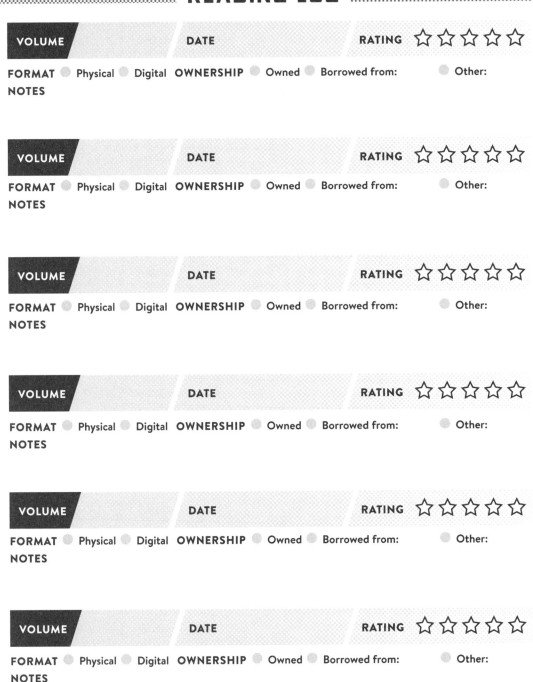

VOLUME   **DATE**   **RATING** ☆ ☆ ☆ ☆ ☆

FORMAT ● Physical ● Digital **OWNERSHIP** ● Owned ● Borrowed from: ● Other:
NOTES

VOLUME   **DATE**   **RATING** ☆ ☆ ☆ ☆ ☆

FORMAT ● Physical ● Digital **OWNERSHIP** ● Owned ● Borrowed from: ● Other:
NOTES

VOLUME   **DATE**   **RATING** ☆ ☆ ☆ ☆ ☆

FORMAT ● Physical ● Digital **OWNERSHIP** ● Owned ● Borrowed from: ● Other:
NOTES

VOLUME   **DATE**   **RATING** ☆ ☆ ☆ ☆ ☆

FORMAT ● Physical ● Digital **OWNERSHIP** ● Owned ● Borrowed from: ● Other:
NOTES

VOLUME   **DATE**   **RATING** ☆ ☆ ☆ ☆ ☆

FORMAT ● Physical ● Digital **OWNERSHIP** ● Owned ● Borrowed from: ● Other:
NOTES

VOLUME   **DATE**   **RATING** ☆ ☆ ☆ ☆ ☆

FORMAT ● Physical ● Digital **OWNERSHIP** ● Owned ● Borrowed from: ● Other:
NOTES

PLOT What hooked you on the plot? What storyline kept/keeps you reading?

What would you have done differently? Where did you want this plot to go?

ART What stood out about the art? How did the art fit the story?

CHARACTERS Who's the most compelling character of the series? The honor of best girl/best boy goes to...

This manga is like (or reminds me of)...

Is there an anime adaptation or film for this manga? If not, do you think there should be one?

Additional notes

📖 MANGA SERIES TRACKER

MANGA TITLE

AUTHOR/MANGAKA

First Volume Publication Date   *Final Volume Publication Date*

GENRE ○ Shōnen ○ Shōjo ○ Seinen ○ Josei ○ Kodomomuke (Children's)

INTEREST(S)

- Action-Adventure
- Comedy
- Drama
- Dystopian
- Family
- Fantasy
- History
- Horror

- Isekai
- LGBTQ+
- Martial Arts
- Mecha
- Music
- Mystery/Thriller
- Parody
- Romance

- School Life
- Sci-Fi
- Slice-of-Life
- Sports
- Supernatural
- Superpower
- Other:

PUBLISHER

SERIES STATUS
- Ongoing
- Complete
- Incomplete

TOTAL VOLUMES IN SERIES

MY STATUS
- Plan to Read
- Started Reading
- Completed
- Dropped

SERIES RATING

AMAZING
☆ 5
☆
☆
☆
☆ 1
APPALLING

READING LOG

VOLUME   **DATE**   **RATING** ☆ ☆ ☆ ☆ ☆

FORMAT ○ Physical ○ Digital **OWNERSHIP** ○ Owned ○ Borrowed from: ○ Other:

NOTES

VOLUME   **DATE**   **RATING** ☆ ☆ ☆ ☆ ☆

FORMAT ○ Physical ○ Digital **OWNERSHIP** ○ Owned ○ Borrowed from: ○ Other:

NOTES

VOLUME   **DATE**   **RATING** ☆ ☆ ☆ ☆ ☆

FORMAT ○ Physical ○ Digital **OWNERSHIP** ○ Owned ○ Borrowed from: ○ Other:

NOTES

VOLUME   **DATE**   **RATING** ☆ ☆ ☆ ☆ ☆

FORMAT ○ Physical ○ Digital **OWNERSHIP** ○ Owned ○ Borrowed from: ○ Other:

NOTES

VOLUME   **DATE**   **RATING** ☆ ☆ ☆ ☆ ☆

FORMAT ○ Physical ○ Digital **OWNERSHIP** ○ Owned ○ Borrowed from: ○ Other:

NOTES

VOLUME   **DATE**   **RATING** ☆ ☆ ☆ ☆ ☆

FORMAT ○ Physical ○ Digital **OWNERSHIP** ○ Owned ○ Borrowed from: ○ Other:

NOTES

READING LOG

VOLUME **DATE** **RATING** ☆☆☆☆☆

FORMAT ● Physical ● Digital **OWNERSHIP** ● Owned ● Borrowed from: ● Other:

NOTES

VOLUME **DATE** **RATING** ☆☆☆☆☆

FORMAT ● Physical ● Digital **OWNERSHIP** ● Owned ● Borrowed from: ● Other:

NOTES

VOLUME **DATE** **RATING** ☆☆☆☆☆

FORMAT ● Physical ● Digital **OWNERSHIP** ● Owned ● Borrowed from: ● Other:

NOTES

VOLUME **DATE** **RATING** ☆☆☆☆☆

FORMAT ● Physical ● Digital **OWNERSHIP** ● Owned ● Borrowed from: ● Other:

NOTES

VOLUME **DATE** **RATING** ☆☆☆☆☆

FORMAT ● Physical ● Digital **OWNERSHIP** ● Owned ● Borrowed from: ● Other:

NOTES

VOLUME **DATE** **RATING** ☆☆☆☆☆

FORMAT ● Physical ● Digital **OWNERSHIP** ● Owned ● Borrowed from: ● Other:

NOTES

VOLUME **DATE** **RATING** ☆ ☆ ☆ ☆ ☆

FORMAT ● Physical ● Digital **OWNERSHIP** ● Owned ● Borrowed from: ● Other:

NOTES

VOLUME **DATE** **RATING** ☆ ☆ ☆ ☆ ☆

FORMAT ● Physical ● Digital **OWNERSHIP** ● Owned ● Borrowed from: ● Other:

NOTES

VOLUME **DATE** **RATING** ☆ ☆ ☆ ☆ ☆

FORMAT ● Physical ● Digital **OWNERSHIP** ● Owned ● Borrowed from: ● Other:

NOTES

VOLUME **DATE** **RATING** ☆ ☆ ☆ ☆ ☆

FORMAT ● Physical ● Digital **OWNERSHIP** ● Owned ● Borrowed from: ● Other:

NOTES

VOLUME **DATE** **RATING** ☆ ☆ ☆ ☆ ☆

FORMAT ● Physical ● Digital **OWNERSHIP** ● Owned ● Borrowed from: ● Other:

NOTES

VOLUME **DATE** **RATING** ☆ ☆ ☆ ☆ ☆

FORMAT ● Physical ● Digital **OWNERSHIP** ● Owned ● Borrowed from: ● Other:

NOTES

PLOT What hooked you on the plot? What storyline kept/keeps you reading?

What would you have done differently? Where did you want this plot to go?

ART What stood out about the art? How did the art fit the story?

CHARACTERS Who's the most compelling character of the series? The honor of best girl/best boy goes to...

This manga is like (or reminds me of)...

Is there an anime adaptation or film for this manga? If not, do you think there should be one?

Additional notes

📖 MANGA SERIES TRACKER

MANGA TITLE

AUTHOR/MANGAKA

First Volume Publication Date

Final Volume Publication Date

GENRE ○ Shōnen ○ Shōjo ○ Seinen ○ Josei ○ Kodomomuke (Children's)

INTEREST(S)

- Action-Adventure
- Comedy
- Drama
- Dystopian
- Family
- Fantasy
- History
- Horror

- Isekai
- LGBTQ+
- Martial Arts
- Mecha
- Music
- Mystery/Thriller
- Parody
- Romance

- School Life
- Sci-Fi
- Slice-of-Life
- Sports
- Supernatural
- Superpower
- Other:

PUBLISHER

SERIES STATUS
- Ongoing
- Complete
- Incomplete

TOTAL VOLUMES IN SERIES

MY STATUS
- Plan to Read
- Started Reading
- Completed
- Dropped

SERIES RATING

AMAZING
☆ 5
☆
☆
☆
☆ 1
APPALLING

READING LOG

VOLUME　　　　　　**DATE**　　　　**RATING** ☆☆☆☆☆

FORMAT ● Physical ● Digital **OWNERSHIP** ● Owned ● Borrowed from:　　　● Other:
NOTES

VOLUME　　　　　　**DATE**　　　　**RATING** ☆☆☆☆☆

FORMAT ● Physical ● Digital **OWNERSHIP** ● Owned ● Borrowed from:　　　● Other:
NOTES

VOLUME　　　　　　**DATE**　　　　**RATING** ☆☆☆☆☆

FORMAT ● Physical ● Digital **OWNERSHIP** ● Owned ● Borrowed from:　　　● Other:
NOTES

VOLUME　　　　　　**DATE**　　　　**RATING** ☆☆☆☆☆

FORMAT ● Physical ● Digital **OWNERSHIP** ● Owned ● Borrowed from:　　　● Other:
NOTES

VOLUME　　　　　　**DATE**　　　　**RATING** ☆☆☆☆☆

FORMAT ● Physical ● Digital **OWNERSHIP** ● Owned ● Borrowed from:　　　● Other:
NOTES

VOLUME　　　　　　**DATE**　　　　**RATING** ☆☆☆☆☆

FORMAT ● Physical ● Digital **OWNERSHIP** ● Owned ● Borrowed from:　　　● Other:
NOTES

READING LOG

VOLUME	DATE	RATING ☆☆☆☆☆

FORMAT ⚬ Physical ⚬ Digital **OWNERSHIP** ⚬ Owned ⚬ Borrowed from: ⚬ Other:
NOTES

VOLUME	DATE	RATING ☆☆☆☆☆

FORMAT ⚬ Physical ⚬ Digital **OWNERSHIP** ⚬ Owned ⚬ Borrowed from: ⚬ Other:
NOTES

VOLUME	DATE	RATING ☆☆☆☆☆

FORMAT ⚬ Physical ⚬ Digital **OWNERSHIP** ⚬ Owned ⚬ Borrowed from: ⚬ Other:
NOTES

VOLUME	DATE	RATING ☆☆☆☆☆

FORMAT ⚬ Physical ⚬ Digital **OWNERSHIP** ⚬ Owned ⚬ Borrowed from: ⚬ Other:
NOTES

VOLUME	DATE	RATING ☆☆☆☆☆

FORMAT ⚬ Physical ⚬ Digital **OWNERSHIP** ⚬ Owned ⚬ Borrowed from: ⚬ Other:
NOTES

VOLUME	DATE	RATING ☆☆☆☆☆

FORMAT ⚬ Physical ⚬ Digital **OWNERSHIP** ⚬ Owned ⚬ Borrowed from: ⚬ Other:
NOTES

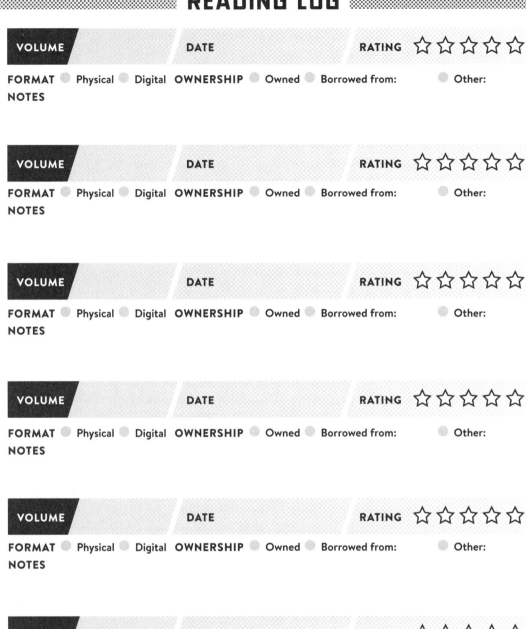

VOLUME **DATE** **RATING** ☆☆☆☆☆

FORMAT ● Physical ● Digital **OWNERSHIP** ● Owned ● Borrowed from: ● Other:

NOTES

VOLUME **DATE** **RATING** ☆☆☆☆☆

FORMAT ● Physical ● Digital **OWNERSHIP** ● Owned ● Borrowed from: ● Other:

NOTES

VOLUME **DATE** **RATING** ☆☆☆☆☆

FORMAT ● Physical ● Digital **OWNERSHIP** ● Owned ● Borrowed from: ● Other:

NOTES

VOLUME **DATE** **RATING** ☆☆☆☆☆

FORMAT ● Physical ● Digital **OWNERSHIP** ● Owned ● Borrowed from: ● Other:

NOTES

VOLUME **DATE** **RATING** ☆☆☆☆☆

FORMAT ● Physical ● Digital **OWNERSHIP** ● Owned ● Borrowed from: ● Other:

NOTES

VOLUME **DATE** **RATING** ☆☆☆☆☆

FORMAT ● Physical ● Digital **OWNERSHIP** ● Owned ● Borrowed from: ● Other:

NOTES

PLOT What hooked you on the plot? What storyline kept/keeps you reading?

What would you have done differently? Where did you want this plot to go?

ART What stood out about the art? How did the art fit the story?

CHARACTERS Who's the most compelling character of the series? The honor of best girl/best boy goes to...

This manga is like (or reminds me of)...

Is there an anime adaptation or film for this manga? If not, do you think there should be one?

Additional notes

📖 MANGA SERIES TRACKER

MANGA TITLE

AUTHOR/MANGAKA

First Volume Publication Date　　　　　　*Final Volume Publication Date*

GENRE　　○ Shōnen　　○ Shōjo　　○ Seinen　　○ Josei　　○ Kodomomuke (Children's)

INTEREST(S)

- Action-Adventure
- Comedy
- Drama
- Dystopian
- Family
- Fantasy
- History
- Horror

- Isekai
- LGBTQ+
- Martial Arts
- Mecha
- Music
- Mystery/Thriller
- Parody
- Romance

- School Life
- Sci-Fi
- Slice-of-Life
- Sports
- Supernatural
- Superpower
- Other:

PUBLISHER

SERIES STATUS

○ Ongoing　　○ Complete　　○ Incomplete

TOTAL VOLUMES IN SERIES

MY STATUS

○ Plan to Read　　○ Completed

○ Started Reading　　○ Dropped

SERIES RATING

AMAZING
☆ 5
☆
☆
☆
☆ 1
APPALLING

READING LOG

VOLUME **DATE** **RATING** ☆☆☆☆☆

FORMAT ◯ Physical ◯ Digital **OWNERSHIP** ◯ Owned ◯ Borrowed from: ◯ Other:
NOTES

VOLUME **DATE** **RATING** ☆☆☆☆☆

FORMAT ◯ Physical ◯ Digital **OWNERSHIP** ◯ Owned ◯ Borrowed from: ◯ Other:
NOTES

VOLUME **DATE** **RATING** ☆☆☆☆☆

FORMAT ◯ Physical ◯ Digital **OWNERSHIP** ◯ Owned ◯ Borrowed from: ◯ Other:
NOTES

VOLUME **DATE** **RATING** ☆☆☆☆☆

FORMAT ◯ Physical ◯ Digital **OWNERSHIP** ◯ Owned ◯ Borrowed from: ◯ Other:
NOTES

VOLUME **DATE** **RATING** ☆☆☆☆☆

FORMAT ◯ Physical ◯ Digital **OWNERSHIP** ◯ Owned ◯ Borrowed from: ◯ Other:
NOTES

VOLUME **DATE** **RATING** ☆☆☆☆☆

FORMAT ◯ Physical ◯ Digital **OWNERSHIP** ◯ Owned ◯ Borrowed from: ◯ Other:
NOTES

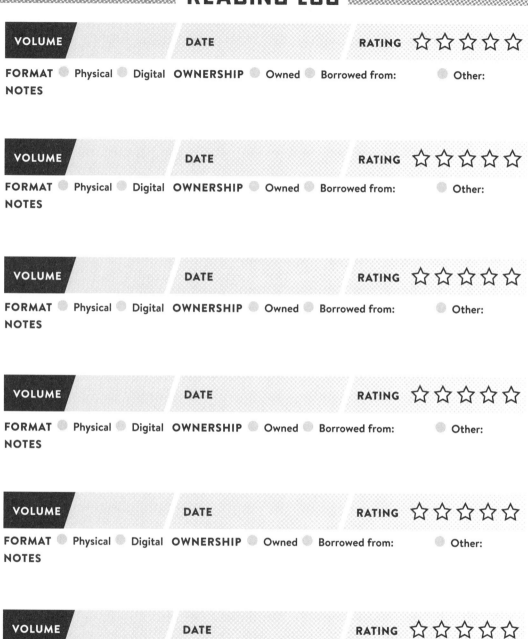

READING LOG

VOLUME **DATE** **RATING** ☆☆☆☆☆

FORMAT ● Physical ● Digital **OWNERSHIP** ● Owned ● Borrowed from: ● Other:
NOTES

VOLUME **DATE** **RATING** ☆☆☆☆☆

FORMAT ● Physical ● Digital **OWNERSHIP** ● Owned ● Borrowed from: ● Other:
NOTES

VOLUME **DATE** **RATING** ☆☆☆☆☆

FORMAT ● Physical ● Digital **OWNERSHIP** ● Owned ● Borrowed from: ● Other:
NOTES

VOLUME **DATE** **RATING** ☆☆☆☆☆

FORMAT ● Physical ● Digital **OWNERSHIP** ● Owned ● Borrowed from: ● Other:
NOTES

VOLUME **DATE** **RATING** ☆☆☆☆☆

FORMAT ● Physical ● Digital **OWNERSHIP** ● Owned ● Borrowed from: ● Other:
NOTES

VOLUME **DATE** **RATING** ☆☆☆☆☆

FORMAT ● Physical ● Digital **OWNERSHIP** ● Owned ● Borrowed from: ● Other:
NOTES

VOLUME **DATE** **RATING** ☆ ☆ ☆ ☆ ☆

FORMAT ● Physical ● Digital **OWNERSHIP** ● Owned ● Borrowed from: ● Other:
NOTES

VOLUME **DATE** **RATING** ☆ ☆ ☆ ☆ ☆

FORMAT ● Physical ● Digital **OWNERSHIP** ● Owned ● Borrowed from: ● Other:
NOTES

VOLUME **DATE** **RATING** ☆ ☆ ☆ ☆ ☆

FORMAT ● Physical ● Digital **OWNERSHIP** ● Owned ● Borrowed from: ● Other:
NOTES

VOLUME **DATE** **RATING** ☆ ☆ ☆ ☆ ☆

FORMAT ● Physical ● Digital **OWNERSHIP** ● Owned ● Borrowed from: ● Other:
NOTES

VOLUME **DATE** **RATING** ☆ ☆ ☆ ☆ ☆

FORMAT ● Physical ● Digital **OWNERSHIP** ● Owned ● Borrowed from: ● Other:
NOTES

VOLUME **DATE** **RATING** ☆ ☆ ☆ ☆ ☆

FORMAT ● Physical ● Digital **OWNERSHIP** ● Owned ● Borrowed from: ● Other:
NOTES

PLOT What hooked you on the plot? What storyline kept/keeps you reading?

What would you have done differently? Where did you want this plot to go?

ART What stood out about the art? How did the art fit the story?

CHARACTERS Who's the most compelling character of the series? The honor of best girl/best boy goes to...

This manga is like (or reminds me of)...

Is there an anime adaptation or film for this manga? If not, do you think there should be one?

Additional notes

📖 MANGA SERIES TRACKER

MANGA TITLE

AUTHOR/MANGAKA

First Volume Publication Date _____   *Final Volume Publication Date* _____

GENRE   ○ Shōnen   ○ Shōjo   ○ Seinen   ○ Josei   ○ Kodomomuke (Children's)

INTEREST(S)

- ○ Action-Adventure
- ○ Comedy
- ○ Drama
- ○ Dystopian
- ○ Family
- ○ Fantasy
- ○ History
- ○ Horror

- ○ Isekai
- ○ LGBTQ+
- ○ Martial Arts
- ○ Mecha
- ○ Music
- ○ Mystery/Thriller
- ○ Parody
- ○ Romance

- ○ School Life
- ○ Sci-Fi
- ○ Slice-of-Life
- ○ Sports
- ○ Supernatural
- ○ Superpower
- ○ Other: _____

PUBLISHER _____

SERIES STATUS
- ○ Ongoing   ○ Complete   ○ Incomplete

TOTAL VOLUMES IN SERIES _____

MY STATUS
- ○ Plan to Read   ○ Completed
- ○ Started Reading   ○ Dropped

SERIES RATING

AMAZING
☆ 5
☆
☆
☆
☆ 1
APPALLING

READING LOG

VOLUME   **DATE**   **RATING** ☆☆☆☆☆

FORMAT ● Physical ● Digital **OWNERSHIP** ● Owned ● Borrowed from: ● Other:

NOTES

VOLUME   **DATE**   **RATING** ☆☆☆☆☆

FORMAT ● Physical ● Digital **OWNERSHIP** ● Owned ● Borrowed from: ● Other:

NOTES

VOLUME   **DATE**   **RATING** ☆☆☆☆☆

FORMAT ● Physical ● Digital **OWNERSHIP** ● Owned ● Borrowed from: ● Other:

NOTES

VOLUME   **DATE**   **RATING** ☆☆☆☆☆

FORMAT ● Physical ● Digital **OWNERSHIP** ● Owned ● Borrowed from: ● Other:

NOTES

VOLUME   **DATE**   **RATING** ☆☆☆☆☆

FORMAT ● Physical ● Digital **OWNERSHIP** ● Owned ● Borrowed from: ● Other:

NOTES

VOLUME   **DATE**   **RATING** ☆☆☆☆☆

FORMAT ● Physical ● Digital **OWNERSHIP** ● Owned ● Borrowed from: ● Other:

NOTES

READING LOG

VOLUME   **DATE**   **RATING** ☆☆☆☆☆

FORMAT ● Physical ● Digital **OWNERSHIP** ● Owned ● Borrowed from: ● Other:
NOTES

VOLUME   **DATE**   **RATING** ☆☆☆☆☆

FORMAT ● Physical ● Digital **OWNERSHIP** ● Owned ● Borrowed from: ● Other:
NOTES

VOLUME   **DATE**   **RATING** ☆☆☆☆☆

FORMAT ● Physical ● Digital **OWNERSHIP** ● Owned ● Borrowed from: ● Other:
NOTES

VOLUME   **DATE**   **RATING** ☆☆☆☆☆

FORMAT ● Physical ● Digital **OWNERSHIP** ● Owned ● Borrowed from: ● Other:
NOTES

VOLUME   **DATE**   **RATING** ☆☆☆☆☆

FORMAT ● Physical ● Digital **OWNERSHIP** ● Owned ● Borrowed from: ● Other:
NOTES

VOLUME   **DATE**   **RATING** ☆☆☆☆☆

FORMAT ● Physical ● Digital **OWNERSHIP** ● Owned ● Borrowed from: ● Other:
NOTES

VOLUME **DATE** **RATING** ☆☆☆☆☆

FORMAT ○ Physical ○ Digital **OWNERSHIP** ○ Owned ○ Borrowed from: ○ Other:

NOTES

VOLUME **DATE** **RATING** ☆☆☆☆☆

FORMAT ○ Physical ○ Digital **OWNERSHIP** ○ Owned ○ Borrowed from: ○ Other:

NOTES

VOLUME **DATE** **RATING** ☆☆☆☆☆

FORMAT ○ Physical ○ Digital **OWNERSHIP** ○ Owned ○ Borrowed from: ○ Other:

NOTES

VOLUME **DATE** **RATING** ☆☆☆☆☆

FORMAT ○ Physical ○ Digital **OWNERSHIP** ○ Owned ○ Borrowed from: ○ Other:

NOTES

VOLUME **DATE** **RATING** ☆☆☆☆☆

FORMAT ○ Physical ○ Digital **OWNERSHIP** ○ Owned ○ Borrowed from: ○ Other:

NOTES

VOLUME **DATE** **RATING** ☆☆☆☆☆

FORMAT ○ Physical ○ Digital **OWNERSHIP** ○ Owned ○ Borrowed from: ○ Other:

NOTES

PLOT What hooked you on the plot? What storyline kept/keeps you reading?

What would you have done differently? Where did you want this plot to go?

ART What stood out about the art? How did the art fit the story?

CHARACTERS Who's the most compelling character of the series? The honor of best girl/best boy goes to...

This manga is like (or reminds me of)...

Is there an anime adaptation or film for this manga? If not, do you think there should be one?

Additional notes

📖 MANGA SERIES TRACKER

MANGA TITLE

AUTHOR/MANGAKA

First Volume Publication Date

Final Volume Publication Date

GENRE   ○ Shōnen   ○ Shōjo   ○ Seinen   ○ Josei   ○ Kodomomuke (Children's)

INTEREST(S)

- ○ Action-Adventure
- ○ Comedy
- ○ Drama
- ○ Dystopian
- ○ Family
- ○ Fantasy
- ○ History
- ○ Horror

- ○ Isekai
- ○ LGBTQ+
- ○ Martial Arts
- ○ Mecha
- ○ Music
- ○ Mystery/Thriller
- ○ Parody
- ○ Romance

- ○ School Life
- ○ Sci-Fi
- ○ Slice-of-Life
- ○ Sports
- ○ Supernatural
- ○ Superpower
- ○ Other:

PUBLISHER

SERIES STATUS

- ○ Ongoing
- ○ Complete
- ○ Incomplete

TOTAL VOLUMES IN SERIES

MY STATUS
- ○ Plan to Read
- ○ Started Reading
- ○ Completed
- ○ Dropped

SERIES RATING

AMAZING

☆ ⑤

☆

☆

☆

☆ ①

APPALLING

READING LOG

VOLUME **DATE** **RATING** ☆☆☆☆☆

FORMAT ● Physical ● Digital **OWNERSHIP** ● Owned ● Borrowed from: ● Other:
NOTES

VOLUME **DATE** **RATING** ☆☆☆☆☆

FORMAT ● Physical ● Digital **OWNERSHIP** ● Owned ● Borrowed from: ● Other:
NOTES

VOLUME **DATE** **RATING** ☆☆☆☆☆

FORMAT ● Physical ● Digital **OWNERSHIP** ● Owned ● Borrowed from: ● Other:
NOTES

VOLUME **DATE** **RATING** ☆☆☆☆☆

FORMAT ● Physical ● Digital **OWNERSHIP** ● Owned ● Borrowed from: ● Other:
NOTES

VOLUME **DATE** **RATING** ☆☆☆☆☆

FORMAT ● Physical ● Digital **OWNERSHIP** ● Owned ● Borrowed from: ● Other:
NOTES

VOLUME **DATE** **RATING** ☆☆☆☆☆

FORMAT ● Physical ● Digital **OWNERSHIP** ● Owned ● Borrowed from: ● Other:
NOTES

READING LOG

VOLUME **DATE** **RATING** ☆☆☆☆☆

FORMAT ○ Physical ○ Digital **OWNERSHIP** ○ Owned ○ Borrowed from: ○ Other:
NOTES

VOLUME **DATE** **RATING** ☆☆☆☆☆

FORMAT ○ Physical ○ Digital **OWNERSHIP** ○ Owned ○ Borrowed from: ○ Other:
NOTES

VOLUME **DATE** **RATING** ☆☆☆☆☆

FORMAT ○ Physical ○ Digital **OWNERSHIP** ○ Owned ○ Borrowed from: ○ Other:
NOTES

VOLUME **DATE** **RATING** ☆☆☆☆☆

FORMAT ○ Physical ○ Digital **OWNERSHIP** ○ Owned ○ Borrowed from: ○ Other:
NOTES

VOLUME **DATE** **RATING** ☆☆☆☆☆

FORMAT ○ Physical ○ Digital **OWNERSHIP** ○ Owned ○ Borrowed from: ○ Other:
NOTES

VOLUME **DATE** **RATING** ☆☆☆☆☆

FORMAT ○ Physical ○ Digital **OWNERSHIP** ○ Owned ○ Borrowed from: ○ Other:
NOTES

VOLUME **DATE** **RATING** ☆☆☆☆☆

FORMAT ● Physical ● Digital **OWNERSHIP** ● Owned ● Borrowed from: ● Other:

NOTES

VOLUME **DATE** **RATING** ☆☆☆☆☆

FORMAT ● Physical ● Digital **OWNERSHIP** ● Owned ● Borrowed from: ● Other:

NOTES

VOLUME **DATE** **RATING** ☆☆☆☆☆

FORMAT ● Physical ● Digital **OWNERSHIP** ● Owned ● Borrowed from: ● Other:

NOTES

VOLUME **DATE** **RATING** ☆☆☆☆☆

FORMAT ● Physical ● Digital **OWNERSHIP** ● Owned ● Borrowed from: ● Other:

NOTES

VOLUME **DATE** **RATING** ☆☆☆☆☆

FORMAT ● Physical ● Digital **OWNERSHIP** ● Owned ● Borrowed from: ● Other:

NOTES

VOLUME **DATE** **RATING** ☆☆☆☆☆

FORMAT ● Physical ● Digital **OWNERSHIP** ● Owned ● Borrowed from: ● Other:

NOTES

PLOT What hooked you on the plot? What storyline kept/keeps you reading?

What would you have done differently? Where did you want this plot to go?

ART What stood out about the art? How did the art fit the story?

CHARACTERS Who's the most compelling character of the series? The honor of best girl/best boy goes to...

This manga is like (or reminds me of)...

Is there an anime adaptation or film for this manga? If not, do you think there should be one?

Additional notes

MANGA SERIES TRACKER

MANGA TITLE

AUTHOR/MANGAKA

First Volume Publication Date

Final Volume Publication Date

GENRE ○ Shōnen ○ Shōjo ○ Seinen ○ Josei ○ Kodomomuke (Children's)

INTEREST(S)

- Action-Adventure
- Comedy
- Drama
- Dystopian
- Family
- Fantasy
- History
- Horror

- Isekai
- LGBTQ+
- Martial Arts
- Mecha
- Music
- Mystery/Thriller
- Parody
- Romance

- School Life
- Sci-Fi
- Slice-of-Life
- Sports
- Supernatural
- Superpower
- Other:

PUBLISHER

SERIES STATUS
- Ongoing
- Complete
- Incomplete

TOTAL VOLUMES IN SERIES

MY STATUS
- Plan to Read
- Started Reading
- Completed
- Dropped

SERIES RATING

AMAZING

☆ 5
☆
☆
☆
☆ 1

APPALLING

READING LOG

VOLUME   **DATE**   **RATING** ☆☆☆☆☆

FORMAT ● Physical ● Digital **OWNERSHIP** ● Owned ● Borrowed from: ● Other:

NOTES

VOLUME   **DATE**   **RATING** ☆☆☆☆☆

FORMAT ● Physical ● Digital **OWNERSHIP** ● Owned ● Borrowed from: ● Other:

NOTES

VOLUME   **DATE**   **RATING** ☆☆☆☆☆

FORMAT ● Physical ● Digital **OWNERSHIP** ● Owned ● Borrowed from: ● Other:

NOTES

VOLUME   **DATE**   **RATING** ☆☆☆☆☆

FORMAT ● Physical ● Digital **OWNERSHIP** ● Owned ● Borrowed from: ● Other:

NOTES

VOLUME   **DATE**   **RATING** ☆☆☆☆☆

FORMAT ● Physical ● Digital **OWNERSHIP** ● Owned ● Borrowed from: ● Other:

NOTES

VOLUME   **DATE**   **RATING** ☆☆☆☆☆

FORMAT ● Physical ● Digital **OWNERSHIP** ● Owned ● Borrowed from: ● Other:

NOTES

READING LOG

VOLUME   **DATE**   **RATING** ☆☆☆☆☆

FORMAT ⚪ Physical ⚪ Digital   **OWNERSHIP** ⚪ Owned ⚪ Borrowed from: ⚪ Other:

NOTES

VOLUME   **DATE**   **RATING** ☆☆☆☆☆

FORMAT ⚪ Physical ⚪ Digital   **OWNERSHIP** ⚪ Owned ⚪ Borrowed from: ⚪ Other:

NOTES

VOLUME   **DATE**   **RATING** ☆☆☆☆☆

FORMAT ⚪ Physical ⚪ Digital   **OWNERSHIP** ⚪ Owned ⚪ Borrowed from: ⚪ Other:

NOTES

VOLUME   **DATE**   **RATING** ☆☆☆☆☆

FORMAT ⚪ Physical ⚪ Digital   **OWNERSHIP** ⚪ Owned ⚪ Borrowed from: ⚪ Other:

NOTES

VOLUME   **DATE**   **RATING** ☆☆☆☆☆

FORMAT ⚪ Physical ⚪ Digital   **OWNERSHIP** ⚪ Owned ⚪ Borrowed from: ⚪ Other:

NOTES

VOLUME   **DATE**   **RATING** ☆☆☆☆☆

FORMAT ⚪ Physical ⚪ Digital   **OWNERSHIP** ⚪ Owned ⚪ Borrowed from: ⚪ Other:

NOTES

VOLUME **DATE** **RATING** ☆☆☆☆☆

FORMAT ○ Physical ○ Digital **OWNERSHIP** ○ Owned ○ Borrowed from: ○ Other:

NOTES

VOLUME **DATE** **RATING** ☆☆☆☆☆

FORMAT ○ Physical ○ Digital **OWNERSHIP** ○ Owned ○ Borrowed from: ○ Other:

NOTES

VOLUME **DATE** **RATING** ☆☆☆☆☆

FORMAT ○ Physical ○ Digital **OWNERSHIP** ○ Owned ○ Borrowed from: ○ Other:

NOTES

VOLUME **DATE** **RATING** ☆☆☆☆☆

FORMAT ○ Physical ○ Digital **OWNERSHIP** ○ Owned ○ Borrowed from: ○ Other:

NOTES

VOLUME **DATE** **RATING** ☆☆☆☆☆

FORMAT ○ Physical ○ Digital **OWNERSHIP** ○ Owned ○ Borrowed from: ○ Other:

NOTES

VOLUME **DATE** **RATING** ☆☆☆☆☆

FORMAT ○ Physical ○ Digital **OWNERSHIP** ○ Owned ○ Borrowed from: ○ Other:

NOTES

PLOT What hooked you on the plot? What storyline kept/keeps you reading?

What would you have done differently? Where did you want this plot to go?

ART What stood out about the art? How did the art fit the story?

CHARACTERS Who's the most compelling character of the series? The honor of best girl/best boy goes to...

This manga is like (or reminds me of)...

Is there an anime adaptation or film for this manga? If not, do you think there should be one?

Additional notes

📖 MANGA SERIES TRACKER

MANGA TITLE

AUTHOR/MANGAKA

First Volume Publication Date

Final Volume Publication Date

GENRE ◯ Shōnen ◯ Shōjo ◯ Seinen ◯ Josei ◯ Kodomomuke (Children's)

INTEREST(S)

- Action-Adventure
- Comedy
- Drama
- Dystopian
- Family
- Fantasy
- History
- Horror

- Isekai
- LGBTQ+
- Martial Arts
- Mecha
- Music
- Mystery/Thriller
- Parody
- Romance

- School Life
- Sci-Fi
- Slice-of-Life
- Sports
- Supernatural
- Superpower
- Other:

PUBLISHER

SERIES STATUS

◯ Ongoing   ◯ Complete   ◯ Incomplete

TOTAL VOLUMES IN SERIES

MY STATUS   ◯ Plan to Read   ◯ Completed
               ◯ Started Reading   ◯ Dropped

SERIES RATING

AMAZING

☆ 5
☆
☆
☆
☆ 1

APPALLING

READING LOG

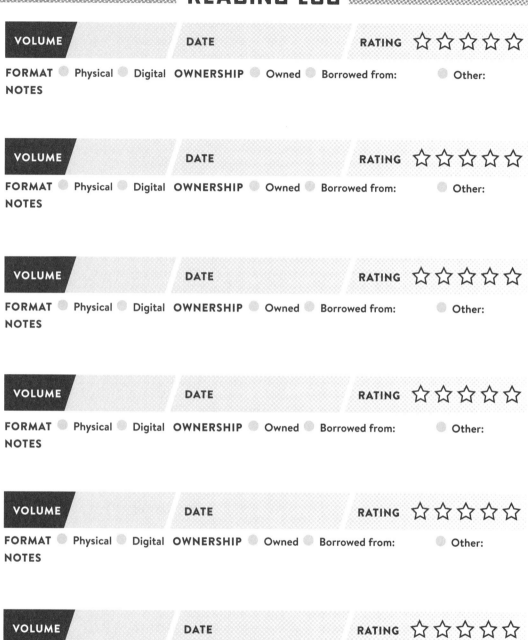

VOLUME **DATE** **RATING** ☆☆☆☆☆
FORMAT ○ Physical ○ Digital **OWNERSHIP** ○ Owned ○ Borrowed from: ○ Other:
NOTES

VOLUME **DATE** **RATING** ☆☆☆☆☆
FORMAT ○ Physical ○ Digital **OWNERSHIP** ○ Owned ○ Borrowed from: ○ Other:
NOTES

VOLUME **DATE** **RATING** ☆☆☆☆☆
FORMAT ○ Physical ○ Digital **OWNERSHIP** ○ Owned ○ Borrowed from: ○ Other:
NOTES

VOLUME **DATE** **RATING** ☆☆☆☆☆
FORMAT ○ Physical ○ Digital **OWNERSHIP** ○ Owned ○ Borrowed from: ○ Other:
NOTES

VOLUME **DATE** **RATING** ☆☆☆☆☆
FORMAT ○ Physical ○ Digital **OWNERSHIP** ○ Owned ○ Borrowed from: ○ Other:
NOTES

VOLUME **DATE** **RATING** ☆☆☆☆☆
FORMAT ○ Physical ○ Digital **OWNERSHIP** ○ Owned ○ Borrowed from: ○ Other:
NOTES

VOLUME   **DATE**   **RATING** ☆☆☆☆☆

FORMAT ○ Physical ○ Digital   **OWNERSHIP** ○ Owned ○ Borrowed from: ○ Other:

NOTES

VOLUME   **DATE**   **RATING** ☆☆☆☆☆

FORMAT ○ Physical ○ Digital   **OWNERSHIP** ○ Owned ○ Borrowed from: ○ Other:

NOTES

VOLUME   **DATE**   **RATING** ☆☆☆☆☆

FORMAT ○ Physical ○ Digital   **OWNERSHIP** ○ Owned ○ Borrowed from: ○ Other:

NOTES

VOLUME   **DATE**   **RATING** ☆☆☆☆☆

FORMAT ○ Physical ○ Digital   **OWNERSHIP** ○ Owned ○ Borrowed from: ○ Other:

NOTES

VOLUME   **DATE**   **RATING** ☆☆☆☆☆

FORMAT ○ Physical ○ Digital   **OWNERSHIP** ○ Owned ○ Borrowed from: ○ Other:

NOTES

VOLUME   **DATE**   **RATING** ☆☆☆☆☆

FORMAT ○ Physical ○ Digital   **OWNERSHIP** ○ Owned ○ Borrowed from: ○ Other:

NOTES

VOLUME **DATE** **RATING** ☆☆☆☆☆

FORMAT ○ Physical ○ Digital **OWNERSHIP** ○ Owned ○ Borrowed from: ○ Other:

NOTES

VOLUME **DATE** **RATING** ☆☆☆☆☆

FORMAT ○ Physical ○ Digital **OWNERSHIP** ○ Owned ○ Borrowed from: ○ Other:

NOTES

VOLUME **DATE** **RATING** ☆☆☆☆☆

FORMAT ○ Physical ○ Digital **OWNERSHIP** ○ Owned ○ Borrowed from: ○ Other:

NOTES

VOLUME **DATE** **RATING** ☆☆☆☆☆

FORMAT ○ Physical ○ Digital **OWNERSHIP** ○ Owned ○ Borrowed from: ○ Other:

NOTES

VOLUME **DATE** **RATING** ☆☆☆☆☆

FORMAT ○ Physical ○ Digital **OWNERSHIP** ○ Owned ○ Borrowed from: ○ Other:

NOTES

VOLUME **DATE** **RATING** ☆☆☆☆☆

FORMAT ○ Physical ○ Digital **OWNERSHIP** ○ Owned ○ Borrowed from: ○ Other:

NOTES

MY SERIES NOTES

PLOT What hooked you on the plot? What storyline kept/keeps you reading?

What would you have done differently? Where did you want this plot to go?

ART What stood out about the art? How did the art fit the story?

CHARACTERS Who's the most compelling character of the series? The honor of best girl/best boy goes to...

This manga is like (or reminds me of)...

Is there an anime adaptation or film for this manga? If not, do you think there should be one?

Additional notes

MANGA TITLE

AUTHOR/MANGAKA

First Volume Publication Date

Final Volume Publication Date

GENRE   ○ Shōnen   ○ Shōjo   ○ Seinen   ○ Josei   ○ Kodomomuke (Children's)

INTEREST(S)

- Action-Adventure
- Comedy
- Drama
- Dystopian
- Family
- Fantasy
- History
- Horror

- Isekai
- LGBTQ+
- Martial Arts
- Mecha
- Music
- Mystery/Thriller
- Parody
- Romance

- School Life
- Sci-Fi
- Slice-of-Life
- Sports
- Supernatural
- Superpower
- Other:

PUBLISHER

SERIES STATUS

○ Ongoing   ○ Complete   ○ Incomplete

TOTAL VOLUMES IN SERIES

MY STATUS   ○ Plan to Read   ○ Completed
○ Started Reading   ○ Dropped

SERIES RATING

AMAZING
☆ 5
☆
☆
☆
☆ 1
APPALLING

READING LOG

VOLUME   **DATE**   **RATING** ☆ ☆ ☆ ☆ ☆

FORMAT ○ Physical ○ Digital **OWNERSHIP** ○ Owned ○ Borrowed from: ○ Other:
NOTES

VOLUME   **DATE**   **RATING** ☆ ☆ ☆ ☆ ☆

FORMAT ○ Physical ○ Digital **OWNERSHIP** ○ Owned ○ Borrowed from: ○ Other:
NOTES

VOLUME   **DATE**   **RATING** ☆ ☆ ☆ ☆ ☆

FORMAT ○ Physical ○ Digital **OWNERSHIP** ○ Owned ○ Borrowed from: ○ Other:
NOTES

VOLUME   **DATE**   **RATING** ☆ ☆ ☆ ☆ ☆

FORMAT ○ Physical ○ Digital **OWNERSHIP** ○ Owned ○ Borrowed from: ○ Other:
NOTES

VOLUME   **DATE**   **RATING** ☆ ☆ ☆ ☆ ☆

FORMAT ○ Physical ○ Digital **OWNERSHIP** ○ Owned ○ Borrowed from: ○ Other:
NOTES

VOLUME   **DATE**   **RATING** ☆ ☆ ☆ ☆ ☆

FORMAT ○ Physical ○ Digital **OWNERSHIP** ○ Owned ○ Borrowed from: ○ Other:
NOTES

READING LOG

VOLUME　　　　　　　　　　**DATE**　　　　　　　　**RATING** ☆☆☆☆☆

FORMAT ○ Physical ○ Digital **OWNERSHIP** ○ Owned ○ Borrowed from: 　 ○ Other:

NOTES

VOLUME　　　　　　　　　　**DATE**　　　　　　　　**RATING** ☆☆☆☆☆

FORMAT ○ Physical ○ Digital **OWNERSHIP** ○ Owned ○ Borrowed from: 　 ○ Other:

NOTES

VOLUME　　　　　　　　　　**DATE**　　　　　　　　**RATING** ☆☆☆☆☆

FORMAT ○ Physical ○ Digital **OWNERSHIP** ○ Owned ○ Borrowed from: 　 ○ Other:

NOTES

VOLUME　　　　　　　　　　**DATE**　　　　　　　　**RATING** ☆☆☆☆☆

FORMAT ○ Physical ○ Digital **OWNERSHIP** ○ Owned ○ Borrowed from: 　 ○ Other:

NOTES

VOLUME　　　　　　　　　　**DATE**　　　　　　　　**RATING** ☆☆☆☆☆

FORMAT ○ Physical ○ Digital **OWNERSHIP** ○ Owned ○ Borrowed from: 　 ○ Other:

NOTES

VOLUME　　　　　　　　　　**DATE**　　　　　　　　**RATING** ☆☆☆☆☆

FORMAT ○ Physical ○ Digital **OWNERSHIP** ○ Owned ○ Borrowed from: 　 ○ Other:

NOTES

VOLUME **DATE** **RATING** ☆☆☆☆☆

FORMAT ○ Physical ○ Digital **OWNERSHIP** ○ Owned ○ Borrowed from: ○ Other:

NOTES

VOLUME **DATE** **RATING** ☆☆☆☆☆

FORMAT ○ Physical ○ Digital **OWNERSHIP** ○ Owned ○ Borrowed from: ○ Other:

NOTES

VOLUME **DATE** **RATING** ☆☆☆☆☆

FORMAT ○ Physical ○ Digital **OWNERSHIP** ○ Owned ○ Borrowed from: ○ Other:

NOTES

VOLUME **DATE** **RATING** ☆☆☆☆☆

FORMAT ○ Physical ○ Digital **OWNERSHIP** ○ Owned ○ Borrowed from: ○ Other:

NOTES

VOLUME **DATE** **RATING** ☆☆☆☆☆

FORMAT ○ Physical ○ Digital **OWNERSHIP** ○ Owned ○ Borrowed from: ○ Other:

NOTES

VOLUME **DATE** **RATING** ☆☆☆☆☆

FORMAT ○ Physical ○ Digital **OWNERSHIP** ○ Owned ○ Borrowed from: ○ Other:

NOTES

PLOT What hooked you on the plot? What storyline kept/keeps you reading?

What would you have done differently? Where did you want this plot to go?

ART What stood out about the art? How did the art fit the story?

CHARACTERS Who's the most compelling character of the series? The honor of best girl/best boy goes to...

This manga is like (or reminds me of)...

Is there an anime adaptation or film for this manga? If not, do you think there should be one?

Additional notes

📖 MANGA SERIES TRACKER

MANGA TITLE

AUTHOR/MANGAKA

First Volume Publication Date   *Final Volume Publication Date*

GENRE ○ Shōnen   ○ Shōjo   ○ Seinen   ○ Josei   ○ Kodomomuke (Children's)

INTEREST(S)

○ Action-Adventure   ○ Isekai   ○ School Life
○ Comedy   ○ LGBTQ+   ○ Sci-Fi
○ Drama   ○ Martial Arts   ○ Slice-of-Life
○ Dystopian   ○ Mecha   ○ Sports
○ Family   ○ Music   ○ Supernatural
○ Fantasy   ○ Mystery/Thriller   ○ Superpower
○ History   ○ Parody   ○ Other:
○ Horror   ○ Romance

PUBLISHER

SERIES STATUS

○ Ongoing   ○ Complete   ○ Incomplete

TOTAL VOLUMES IN SERIES

MY STATUS   ○ Plan to Read   ○ Completed
                ○ Started Reading   ○ Dropped

SERIES RATING

AMAZING
☆ 5
☆
☆
☆
☆ 1
APPALLING

READING LOG

VOLUME　　　　　**DATE**　　　　　**RATING** ☆☆☆☆☆

FORMAT ⬤ Physical ⬤ Digital **OWNERSHIP** ⬤ Owned ⬤ Borrowed from: ⬤ Other:

NOTES

VOLUME　　　　　**DATE**　　　　　**RATING** ☆☆☆☆☆

FORMAT ⬤ Physical ⬤ Digital **OWNERSHIP** ⬤ Owned ⬤ Borrowed from: ⬤ Other:

NOTES

VOLUME　　　　　**DATE**　　　　　**RATING** ☆☆☆☆☆

FORMAT ⬤ Physical ⬤ Digital **OWNERSHIP** ⬤ Owned ⬤ Borrowed from: ⬤ Other:

NOTES

VOLUME　　　　　**DATE**　　　　　**RATING** ☆☆☆☆☆

FORMAT ⬤ Physical ⬤ Digital **OWNERSHIP** ⬤ Owned ⬤ Borrowed from: ⬤ Other:

NOTES

VOLUME　　　　　**DATE**　　　　　**RATING** ☆☆☆☆☆

FORMAT ⬤ Physical ⬤ Digital **OWNERSHIP** ⬤ Owned ⬤ Borrowed from: ⬤ Other:

NOTES

VOLUME　　　　　**DATE**　　　　　**RATING** ☆☆☆☆☆

FORMAT ⬤ Physical ⬤ Digital **OWNERSHIP** ⬤ Owned ⬤ Borrowed from: ⬤ Other:

NOTES

READING LOG

VOLUME **DATE** **RATING** ☆☆☆☆☆

FORMAT ○ Physical ○ Digital **OWNERSHIP** ○ Owned ○ Borrowed from: ○ Other:
NOTES

VOLUME **DATE** **RATING** ☆☆☆☆☆

FORMAT ○ Physical ○ Digital **OWNERSHIP** ○ Owned ○ Borrowed from: ○ Other:
NOTES

VOLUME **DATE** **RATING** ☆☆☆☆☆

FORMAT ○ Physical ○ Digital **OWNERSHIP** ○ Owned ○ Borrowed from: ○ Other:
NOTES

VOLUME **DATE** **RATING** ☆☆☆☆☆

FORMAT ○ Physical ○ Digital **OWNERSHIP** ○ Owned ○ Borrowed from: ○ Other:
NOTES

VOLUME **DATE** **RATING** ☆☆☆☆☆

FORMAT ○ Physical ○ Digital **OWNERSHIP** ○ Owned ○ Borrowed from: ○ Other:
NOTES

VOLUME **DATE** **RATING** ☆☆☆☆☆

FORMAT ○ Physical ○ Digital **OWNERSHIP** ○ Owned ○ Borrowed from: ○ Other:
NOTES

VOLUME **DATE** **RATING** ☆☆☆☆☆

FORMAT ● Physical ● Digital **OWNERSHIP** ● Owned ● Borrowed from: ● Other:
NOTES

VOLUME **DATE** **RATING** ☆☆☆☆☆

FORMAT ● Physical ● Digital **OWNERSHIP** ● Owned ● Borrowed from: ● Other:
NOTES

VOLUME **DATE** **RATING** ☆☆☆☆☆

FORMAT ● Physical ● Digital **OWNERSHIP** ● Owned ● Borrowed from: ● Other:
NOTES

VOLUME **DATE** **RATING** ☆☆☆☆☆

FORMAT ● Physical ● Digital **OWNERSHIP** ● Owned ● Borrowed from: ● Other:
NOTES

VOLUME **DATE** **RATING** ☆☆☆☆☆

FORMAT ● Physical ● Digital **OWNERSHIP** ● Owned ● Borrowed from: ● Other:
NOTES

VOLUME **DATE** **RATING** ☆☆☆☆☆

FORMAT ● Physical ● Digital **OWNERSHIP** ● Owned ● Borrowed from: ● Other:
NOTES

MY SERIES NOTES

PLOT What hooked you on the plot? What storyline kept/keeps you reading?

What would you have done differently? Where did you want this plot to go?

ART What stood out about the art? How did the art fit the story?

CHARACTERS Who's the most compelling character of the series? The honor of best girl/best boy goes to...

This manga is like (or reminds me of)...

Is there an anime adaptation or film for this manga? If not, do you think there should be one?

Additional notes

📖 MANGA SERIES TRACKER

MANGA TITLE

AUTHOR/MANGAKA

First Volume Publication Date

Final Volume Publication Date

GENRE   ○ Shōnen   ○ Shōjo   ○ Seinen   ○ Josei   ○ Kodomomuke (Children's)

INTEREST(S)

- Action-Adventure
- Comedy
- Drama
- Dystopian
- Family
- Fantasy
- History
- Horror

- Isekai
- LGBTQ+
- Martial Arts
- Mecha
- Music
- Mystery/Thriller
- Parody
- Romance

- School Life
- Sci-Fi
- Slice-of-Life
- Sports
- Supernatural
- Superpower
- Other:

PUBLISHER

SERIES STATUS

○ Ongoing   ○ Complete   ○ Incomplete

TOTAL VOLUMES IN SERIES

MY STATUS   ○ Plan to Read   ○ Completed
                ○ Started Reading   ○ Dropped

SERIES RATING

AMAZING

☆ 5
☆
☆
☆
☆ 1

APPALLING

READING LOG

VOLUME **DATE** **RATING** ☆☆☆☆☆

FORMAT ● Physical ● Digital **OWNERSHIP** ● Owned ● Borrowed from: ● Other:

NOTES

VOLUME **DATE** **RATING** ☆☆☆☆☆

FORMAT ● Physical ● Digital **OWNERSHIP** ● Owned ● Borrowed from: ● Other:

NOTES

VOLUME **DATE** **RATING** ☆☆☆☆☆

FORMAT ● Physical ● Digital **OWNERSHIP** ● Owned ● Borrowed from: ● Other:

NOTES

VOLUME **DATE** **RATING** ☆☆☆☆☆

FORMAT ● Physical ● Digital **OWNERSHIP** ● Owned ● Borrowed from: ● Other:

NOTES

VOLUME **DATE** **RATING** ☆☆☆☆☆

FORMAT ● Physical ● Digital **OWNERSHIP** ● Owned ● Borrowed from: ● Other:

NOTES

VOLUME **DATE** **RATING** ☆☆☆☆☆

FORMAT ● Physical ● Digital **OWNERSHIP** ● Owned ● Borrowed from: ● Other:

NOTES

READING LOG

VOLUME   **DATE**   **RATING** ☆☆☆☆☆

FORMAT ○ Physical ○ Digital   **OWNERSHIP** ○ Owned ○ Borrowed from: ○ Other:

NOTES

VOLUME   **DATE**   **RATING** ☆☆☆☆☆

FORMAT ○ Physical ○ Digital   **OWNERSHIP** ○ Owned ○ Borrowed from: ○ Other:

NOTES

VOLUME   **DATE**   **RATING** ☆☆☆☆☆

FORMAT ○ Physical ○ Digital   **OWNERSHIP** ○ Owned ○ Borrowed from: ○ Other:

NOTES

VOLUME   **DATE**   **RATING** ☆☆☆☆☆

FORMAT ○ Physical ○ Digital   **OWNERSHIP** ○ Owned ○ Borrowed from: ○ Other:

NOTES

VOLUME   **DATE**   **RATING** ☆☆☆☆☆

FORMAT ○ Physical ○ Digital   **OWNERSHIP** ○ Owned ○ Borrowed from: ○ Other:

NOTES

VOLUME   **DATE**   **RATING** ☆☆☆☆☆

FORMAT ○ Physical ○ Digital   **OWNERSHIP** ○ Owned ○ Borrowed from: ○ Other:

NOTES

VOLUME **DATE** **RATING** ☆☆☆☆☆

FORMAT ● Physical ● Digital **OWNERSHIP** ● Owned ● Borrowed from: ● Other:
NOTES

VOLUME **DATE** **RATING** ☆☆☆☆☆

FORMAT ● Physical ● Digital **OWNERSHIP** ● Owned ● Borrowed from: ● Other:
NOTES

VOLUME **DATE** **RATING** ☆☆☆☆☆

FORMAT ● Physical ● Digital **OWNERSHIP** ● Owned ● Borrowed from: ● Other:
NOTES

VOLUME **DATE** **RATING** ☆☆☆☆☆

FORMAT ● Physical ● Digital **OWNERSHIP** ● Owned ● Borrowed from: ● Other:
NOTES

VOLUME **DATE** **RATING** ☆☆☆☆☆

FORMAT ● Physical ● Digital **OWNERSHIP** ● Owned ● Borrowed from: ● Other:
NOTES

VOLUME **DATE** **RATING** ☆☆☆☆☆

FORMAT ● Physical ● Digital **OWNERSHIP** ● Owned ● Borrowed from: ● Other:
NOTES

PLOT What hooked you on the plot? What storyline kept/keeps you reading?

What would you have done differently? Where did you want this plot to go?

ART What stood out about the art? How did the art fit the story?

CHARACTERS Who's the most compelling character of the series? The honor of best girl/best boy goes to...

This manga is like (or reminds me of)...

Is there an anime adaptation or film for this manga? If not, do you think there should be one?

Additional notes

📖 MANGA SERIES TRACKER

MANGA TITLE

AUTHOR/MANGAKA

First Volume Publication Date   *Final Volume Publication Date*

GENRE   Shōnen   Shōjo   Seinen   Josei   Kodomomuke (Children's)

INTEREST(S)

- Action-Adventure
- Comedy
- Drama
- Dystopian
- Family
- Fantasy
- History
- Horror

- Isekai
- LGBTQ+
- Martial Arts
- Mecha
- Music
- Mystery/Thriller
- Parody
- Romance

- School Life
- Sci-Fi
- Slice-of-Life
- Sports
- Supernatural
- Superpower
- Other:

PUBLISHER

SERIES STATUS
- Ongoing
- Complete
- Incomplete

TOTAL VOLUMES IN SERIES

MY STATUS
- Plan to Read
- Started Reading
- Completed
- Dropped

SERIES RATING

AMAZING
☆ 5
☆
☆
☆
☆ 1
APPALLING

READING LOG

VOLUME   **DATE**   **RATING** ☆☆☆☆☆

FORMAT ● Physical ● Digital   **OWNERSHIP** ● Owned ● Borrowed from: ● Other:

NOTES

VOLUME   **DATE**   **RATING** ☆☆☆☆☆

FORMAT ● Physical ● Digital   **OWNERSHIP** ● Owned ● Borrowed from: ● Other:

NOTES

VOLUME   **DATE**   **RATING** ☆☆☆☆☆

FORMAT ● Physical ● Digital   **OWNERSHIP** ● Owned ● Borrowed from: ● Other:

NOTES

VOLUME   **DATE**   **RATING** ☆☆☆☆☆

FORMAT ● Physical ● Digital   **OWNERSHIP** ● Owned ● Borrowed from: ● Other:

NOTES

VOLUME   **DATE**   **RATING** ☆☆☆☆☆

FORMAT ● Physical ● Digital   **OWNERSHIP** ● Owned ● Borrowed from: ● Other:

NOTES

VOLUME   **DATE**   **RATING** ☆☆☆☆☆

FORMAT ● Physical ● Digital   **OWNERSHIP** ● Owned ● Borrowed from: ● Other:

NOTES

READING LOG

VOLUME   **DATE**   **RATING** ☆ ☆ ☆ ☆ ☆

FORMAT ○ Physical ○ Digital   **OWNERSHIP** ○ Owned ○ Borrowed from: ○ Other:

NOTES

VOLUME   **DATE**   **RATING** ☆ ☆ ☆ ☆ ☆

FORMAT ○ Physical ○ Digital   **OWNERSHIP** ○ Owned ○ Borrowed from: ○ Other:

NOTES

VOLUME   **DATE**   **RATING** ☆ ☆ ☆ ☆ ☆

FORMAT ○ Physical ○ Digital   **OWNERSHIP** ○ Owned ○ Borrowed from: ○ Other:

NOTES

VOLUME   **DATE**   **RATING** ☆ ☆ ☆ ☆ ☆

FORMAT ○ Physical ○ Digital   **OWNERSHIP** ○ Owned ○ Borrowed from: ○ Other:

NOTES

VOLUME   **DATE**   **RATING** ☆ ☆ ☆ ☆ ☆

FORMAT ○ Physical ○ Digital   **OWNERSHIP** ○ Owned ○ Borrowed from: ○ Other:

NOTES

VOLUME   **DATE**   **RATING** ☆ ☆ ☆ ☆ ☆

FORMAT ○ Physical ○ Digital   **OWNERSHIP** ○ Owned ○ Borrowed from: ○ Other:

NOTES

VOLUME   **DATE**   **RATING** ☆☆☆☆☆

FORMAT ⬤ Physical ⬤ Digital   **OWNERSHIP** ⬤ Owned ⬤ Borrowed from: ⬤ Other:

NOTES

VOLUME   **DATE**   **RATING** ☆☆☆☆☆

FORMAT ⬤ Physical ⬤ Digital   **OWNERSHIP** ⬤ Owned ⬤ Borrowed from: ⬤ Other:

NOTES

VOLUME   **DATE**   **RATING** ☆☆☆☆☆

FORMAT ⬤ Physical ⬤ Digital   **OWNERSHIP** ⬤ Owned ⬤ Borrowed from: ⬤ Other:

NOTES

VOLUME   **DATE**   **RATING** ☆☆☆☆☆

FORMAT ⬤ Physical ⬤ Digital   **OWNERSHIP** ⬤ Owned ⬤ Borrowed from: ⬤ Other:

NOTES

VOLUME   **DATE**   **RATING** ☆☆☆☆☆

FORMAT ⬤ Physical ⬤ Digital   **OWNERSHIP** ⬤ Owned ⬤ Borrowed from: ⬤ Other:

NOTES

VOLUME   **DATE**   **RATING** ☆☆☆☆☆

FORMAT ⬤ Physical ⬤ Digital   **OWNERSHIP** ⬤ Owned ⬤ Borrowed from: ⬤ Other:

NOTES

PLOT What hooked you on the plot? What storyline kept/keeps you reading?

What would you have done differently? Where did you want this plot to go?

ART What stood out about the art? How did the art fit the story?

CHARACTERS Who's the most compelling character of the series? The honor of best girl/best boy goes to...

This manga is like (or reminds me of)...

Is there an anime adaptation or film for this manga? If not, do you think there should be one?

Additional notes

MANGA SERIES TRACKER

MANGA TITLE

AUTHOR/MANGAKA

First Volume Publication Date

Final Volume Publication Date

GENRE ○ Shōnen ○ Shōjo ○ Seinen ○ Josei ○ Kodomomuke (Children's)

INTEREST(S)

- ○ Action-Adventure
- ○ Comedy
- ○ Drama
- ○ Dystopian
- ○ Family
- ○ Fantasy
- ○ History
- ○ Horror

- ○ Isekai
- ○ LGBTQ+
- ○ Martial Arts
- ○ Mecha
- ○ Music
- ○ Mystery/Thriller
- ○ Parody
- ○ Romance

- ○ School Life
- ○ Sci-Fi
- ○ Slice-of-Life
- ○ Sports
- ○ Supernatural
- ○ Superpower
- ○ Other:

PUBLISHER

SERIES STATUS

○ Ongoing ○ Complete ○ Incomplete

TOTAL VOLUMES IN SERIES

MY STATUS ○ Plan to Read ○ Completed
○ Started Reading ○ Dropped

SERIES RATING

AMAGING ☆ ⑤

☆

☆

☆

☆ ①

APPALLING

READING LOG

VOLUME   **DATE**   **RATING** ☆☆☆☆☆

FORMAT ○ Physical ○ Digital   **OWNERSHIP** ○ Owned ○ Borrowed from: ○ Other:

NOTES

VOLUME   **DATE**   **RATING** ☆☆☆☆☆

FORMAT ○ Physical ○ Digital   **OWNERSHIP** ○ Owned ○ Borrowed from: ○ Other:

NOTES

VOLUME   **DATE**   **RATING** ☆☆☆☆☆

FORMAT ○ Physical ○ Digital   **OWNERSHIP** ○ Owned ○ Borrowed from: ○ Other:

NOTES

VOLUME   **DATE**   **RATING** ☆☆☆☆☆

FORMAT ○ Physical ○ Digital   **OWNERSHIP** ○ Owned ○ Borrowed from: ○ Other:

NOTES

VOLUME   **DATE**   **RATING** ☆☆☆☆☆

FORMAT ○ Physical ○ Digital   **OWNERSHIP** ○ Owned ○ Borrowed from: ○ Other:

NOTES

VOLUME   **DATE**   **RATING** ☆☆☆☆☆

FORMAT ○ Physical ○ Digital   **OWNERSHIP** ○ Owned ○ Borrowed from: ○ Other:

NOTES

READING LOG

VOLUME **DATE** **RATING** ☆☆☆☆☆

FORMAT ○ Physical ○ Digital **OWNERSHIP** ○ Owned ○ Borrowed from: ○ Other:

NOTES

VOLUME **DATE** **RATING** ☆☆☆☆☆

FORMAT ○ Physical ○ Digital **OWNERSHIP** ○ Owned ○ Borrowed from: ○ Other:

NOTES

VOLUME **DATE** **RATING** ☆☆☆☆☆

FORMAT ○ Physical ○ Digital **OWNERSHIP** ○ Owned ○ Borrowed from: ○ Other:

NOTES

VOLUME **DATE** **RATING** ☆☆☆☆☆

FORMAT ○ Physical ○ Digital **OWNERSHIP** ○ Owned ○ Borrowed from: ○ Other:

NOTES

VOLUME **DATE** **RATING** ☆☆☆☆☆

FORMAT ○ Physical ○ Digital **OWNERSHIP** ○ Owned ○ Borrowed from: ○ Other:

NOTES

VOLUME **DATE** **RATING** ☆☆☆☆☆

FORMAT ○ Physical ○ Digital **OWNERSHIP** ○ Owned ○ Borrowed from: ○ Other:

NOTES

VOLUME **DATE** **RATING** ☆☆☆☆☆

FORMAT ○ Physical ○ Digital **OWNERSHIP** ○ Owned ○ Borrowed from: ○ Other:

NOTES

VOLUME **DATE** **RATING** ☆☆☆☆☆

FORMAT ○ Physical ○ Digital **OWNERSHIP** ○ Owned ○ Borrowed from: ○ Other:

NOTES

VOLUME **DATE** **RATING** ☆☆☆☆☆

FORMAT ○ Physical ○ Digital **OWNERSHIP** ○ Owned ○ Borrowed from: ○ Other:

NOTES

VOLUME **DATE** **RATING** ☆☆☆☆☆

FORMAT ○ Physical ○ Digital **OWNERSHIP** ○ Owned ○ Borrowed from: ○ Other:

NOTES

VOLUME **DATE** **RATING** ☆☆☆☆☆

FORMAT ○ Physical ○ Digital **OWNERSHIP** ○ Owned ○ Borrowed from: ○ Other:

NOTES

VOLUME **DATE** **RATING** ☆☆☆☆☆

FORMAT ○ Physical ○ Digital **OWNERSHIP** ○ Owned ○ Borrowed from: ○ Other:

NOTES

PLOT What hooked you on the plot? What storyline kept/keeps you reading?

What would you have done differently? Where did you want this plot to go?

ART What stood out about the art? How did the art fit the story?

CHARACTERS Who's the most compelling character of the series? The honor of best girl/best boy goes to...

This manga is like (or reminds me of)...

Is there an anime adaptation or film for this manga? If not, do you think there should be one?

Additional notes

📖 MANGA SERIES TRACKER

MANGA TITLE

AUTHOR/MANGAKA

First Volume Publication Date _____   *Final Volume Publication Date* _____

GENRE ○ Shōnen ○ Shōjo ○ Seinen ○ Josei ○ Kodomomuke (Children's)

INTEREST(S)

- ○ Action-Adventure
- ○ Comedy
- ○ Drama
- ○ Dystopian
- ○ Family
- ○ Fantasy
- ○ History
- ○ Horror

- ○ Isekai
- ○ LGBTQ+
- ○ Martial Arts
- ○ Mecha
- ○ Music
- ○ Mystery/Thriller
- ○ Parody
- ○ Romance

- ○ School Life
- ○ Sci-Fi
- ○ Slice-of-Life
- ○ Sports
- ○ Supernatural
- ○ Superpower
- ○ Other: _____

PUBLISHER _____

SERIES STATUS
- ○ Ongoing   ○ Complete   ○ Incomplete

TOTAL VOLUMES IN SERIES _____

MY STATUS
- ○ Plan to Read   ○ Completed
- ○ Started Reading   ○ Dropped

SERIES RATING

AMAZING
☆ 5
☆
☆
☆
☆ 1
APPALLING

READING LOG

VOLUME   **DATE**   **RATING** ☆☆☆☆☆

FORMAT ● Physical ● Digital **OWNERSHIP** ● Owned ● Borrowed from: ● Other:
NOTES

VOLUME   **DATE**   **RATING** ☆☆☆☆☆

FORMAT ● Physical ● Digital **OWNERSHIP** ● Owned ● Borrowed from: ● Other:
NOTES

VOLUME   **DATE**   **RATING** ☆☆☆☆☆

FORMAT ● Physical ● Digital **OWNERSHIP** ● Owned ● Borrowed from: ● Other:
NOTES

VOLUME   **DATE**   **RATING** ☆☆☆☆☆

FORMAT ● Physical ● Digital **OWNERSHIP** ● Owned ● Borrowed from: ● Other:
NOTES

VOLUME   **DATE**   **RATING** ☆☆☆☆☆

FORMAT ● Physical ● Digital **OWNERSHIP** ● Owned ● Borrowed from: ● Other:
NOTES

VOLUME   **DATE**   **RATING** ☆☆☆☆☆

FORMAT ● Physical ● Digital **OWNERSHIP** ● Owned ● Borrowed from: ● Other:
NOTES

READING LOG

VOLUME   **DATE**   **RATING** ☆☆☆☆☆

FORMAT ○ Physical ○ Digital **OWNERSHIP** ○ Owned ○ Borrowed from: ○ Other:

NOTES

VOLUME   **DATE**   **RATING** ☆☆☆☆☆

FORMAT ○ Physical ○ Digital **OWNERSHIP** ○ Owned ○ Borrowed from: ○ Other:

NOTES

VOLUME   **DATE**   **RATING** ☆☆☆☆☆

FORMAT ○ Physical ○ Digital **OWNERSHIP** ○ Owned ○ Borrowed from: ○ Other:

NOTES

VOLUME   **DATE**   **RATING** ☆☆☆☆☆

FORMAT ○ Physical ○ Digital **OWNERSHIP** ○ Owned ○ Borrowed from: ○ Other:

NOTES

VOLUME   **DATE**   **RATING** ☆☆☆☆☆

FORMAT ○ Physical ○ Digital **OWNERSHIP** ○ Owned ○ Borrowed from: ○ Other:

NOTES

VOLUME   **DATE**   **RATING** ☆☆☆☆☆

FORMAT ○ Physical ○ Digital **OWNERSHIP** ○ Owned ○ Borrowed from: ○ Other:

NOTES

VOLUME **DATE** **RATING** ☆☆☆☆☆

FORMAT ○ Physical ○ Digital **OWNERSHIP** ○ Owned ○ Borrowed from: ○ Other:

NOTES

VOLUME **DATE** **RATING** ☆☆☆☆☆

FORMAT ○ Physical ○ Digital **OWNERSHIP** ○ Owned ○ Borrowed from: ○ Other:

NOTES

VOLUME **DATE** **RATING** ☆☆☆☆☆

FORMAT ○ Physical ○ Digital **OWNERSHIP** ○ Owned ○ Borrowed from: ○ Other:

NOTES

VOLUME **DATE** **RATING** ☆☆☆☆☆

FORMAT ○ Physical ○ Digital **OWNERSHIP** ○ Owned ○ Borrowed from: ○ Other:

NOTES

VOLUME **DATE** **RATING** ☆☆☆☆☆

FORMAT ○ Physical ○ Digital **OWNERSHIP** ○ Owned ○ Borrowed from: ○ Other:

NOTES

VOLUME **DATE** **RATING** ☆☆☆☆☆

FORMAT ○ Physical ○ Digital **OWNERSHIP** ○ Owned ○ Borrowed from: ○ Other:

NOTES

MY SERIES NOTES

PLOT What hooked you on the plot? What storyline kept/keeps you reading?

What would you have done differently? Where did you want this plot to go?

ART What stood out about the art? How did the art fit the story?

CHARACTERS Who's the most compelling character of the series? The honor of best girl/best boy goes to...

This manga is like (or reminds me of)...

Is there an anime adaptation or film for this manga? If not, do you think there should be one?

Additional notes

MANGA TITLE

AUTHOR/MANGAKA

First Volume Publication Date

Final Volume Publication Date

GENRE ○ Shōnen ○ Shōjo ○ Seinen ○ Josei ○ Kodomomuke (Children's)

INTEREST(S)

○ Action-Adventure
○ Comedy
○ Drama
○ Dystopian
○ Family
○ Fantasy
○ History
○ Horror

○ Isekai
○ LGBTQ+
○ Martial Arts
○ Mecha
○ Music
○ Mystery/Thriller
○ Parody
○ Romance

○ School Life
○ Sci-Fi
○ Slice-of-Life
○ Sports
○ Supernatural
○ Superpower
○ Other:

PUBLISHER

SERIES STATUS
○ Ongoing ○ Complete ○ Incomplete

TOTAL VOLUMES IN SERIES

MY STATUS
○ Plan to Read ○ Completed
○ Started Reading ○ Dropped

SERIES RATING

AMAZING
☆ 5
☆
☆
☆
☆ 1
APPALLING

READING LOG

VOLUME | **DATE** | **RATING** ☆☆☆☆☆

FORMAT ○ Physical ○ Digital **OWNERSHIP** ○ Owned ○ Borrowed from: ○ Other:

NOTES

VOLUME | **DATE** | **RATING** ☆☆☆☆☆

FORMAT ○ Physical ○ Digital **OWNERSHIP** ○ Owned ○ Borrowed from: ○ Other:

NOTES

VOLUME | **DATE** | **RATING** ☆☆☆☆☆

FORMAT ○ Physical ○ Digital **OWNERSHIP** ○ Owned ○ Borrowed from: ○ Other:

NOTES

VOLUME | **DATE** | **RATING** ☆☆☆☆☆

FORMAT ○ Physical ○ Digital **OWNERSHIP** ○ Owned ○ Borrowed from: ○ Other:

NOTES

VOLUME | **DATE** | **RATING** ☆☆☆☆☆

FORMAT ○ Physical ○ Digital **OWNERSHIP** ○ Owned ○ Borrowed from: ○ Other:

NOTES

VOLUME | **DATE** | **RATING** ☆☆☆☆☆

FORMAT ○ Physical ○ Digital **OWNERSHIP** ○ Owned ○ Borrowed from: ○ Other:

NOTES

READING LOG

VOLUME **DATE** **RATING** ☆☆☆☆☆

FORMAT ○ Physical ○ Digital **OWNERSHIP** ○ Owned ○ Borrowed from: ○ Other:
NOTES

VOLUME **DATE** **RATING** ☆☆☆☆☆

FORMAT ○ Physical ○ Digital **OWNERSHIP** ○ Owned ○ Borrowed from: ○ Other:
NOTES

VOLUME **DATE** **RATING** ☆☆☆☆☆

FORMAT ○ Physical ○ Digital **OWNERSHIP** ○ Owned ○ Borrowed from: ○ Other:
NOTES

VOLUME **DATE** **RATING** ☆☆☆☆☆

FORMAT ○ Physical ○ Digital **OWNERSHIP** ○ Owned ○ Borrowed from: ○ Other:
NOTES

VOLUME **DATE** **RATING** ☆☆☆☆☆

FORMAT ○ Physical ○ Digital **OWNERSHIP** ○ Owned ○ Borrowed from: ○ Other:
NOTES

VOLUME **DATE** **RATING** ☆☆☆☆☆

FORMAT ○ Physical ○ Digital **OWNERSHIP** ○ Owned ○ Borrowed from: ○ Other:
NOTES

VOLUME   **DATE**   **RATING** ☆☆☆☆☆

FORMAT ⬤ Physical ⬤ Digital   **OWNERSHIP** ⬤ Owned ⬤ Borrowed from: ⬤ Other:

NOTES

VOLUME   **DATE**   **RATING** ☆☆☆☆☆

FORMAT ⬤ Physical ⬤ Digital   **OWNERSHIP** ⬤ Owned ⬤ Borrowed from: ⬤ Other:

NOTES

VOLUME   **DATE**   **RATING** ☆☆☆☆☆

FORMAT ⬤ Physical ⬤ Digital   **OWNERSHIP** ⬤ Owned ⬤ Borrowed from: ⬤ Other:

NOTES

VOLUME   **DATE**   **RATING** ☆☆☆☆☆

FORMAT ⬤ Physical ⬤ Digital   **OWNERSHIP** ⬤ Owned ⬤ Borrowed from: ⬤ Other:

NOTES

VOLUME   **DATE**   **RATING** ☆☆☆☆☆

FORMAT ⬤ Physical ⬤ Digital   **OWNERSHIP** ⬤ Owned ⬤ Borrowed from: ⬤ Other:

NOTES

VOLUME   **DATE**   **RATING** ☆☆☆☆☆

FORMAT ⬤ Physical ⬤ Digital   **OWNERSHIP** ⬤ Owned ⬤ Borrowed from: ⬤ Other:

NOTES

PLOT What hooked you on the plot? What storyline kept/keeps you reading?

What would you have done differently? Where did you want this plot to go?

ART What stood out about the art? How did the art fit the story?

CHARACTERS Who's the most compelling character of the series? The honor of best girl/best boy goes to...

This manga is like (or reminds me of)...

Is there an anime adaptation or film for this manga? If not, do you think there should be one?

Additional notes

📖 MANGA SERIES TRACKER

MANGA TITLE

AUTHOR/MANGAKA

First Volume Publication Date

Final Volume Publication Date

GENRE ○ Shōnen ○ Shōjo ○ Seinen ○ Josei ○ Kodomomuke (Children's)

INTEREST(S)

○ Action-Adventure ○ Isekai ○ School Life

○ Comedy ○ LGBTQ+ ○ Sci-Fi

○ Drama ○ Martial Arts ○ Slice-of-Life

○ Dystopian ○ Mecha ○ Sports

○ Family ○ Music ○ Supernatural

○ Fantasy ○ Mystery/Thriller ○ Superpower

○ History ○ Parody ○ Other:

○ Horror ○ Romance

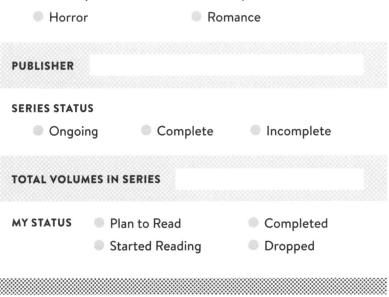

PUBLISHER

SERIES STATUS

○ Ongoing ○ Complete ○ Incomplete

TOTAL VOLUMES IN SERIES

MY STATUS ○ Plan to Read ○ Completed

○ Started Reading ○ Dropped

SERIES RATING

AMAZING

☆ 5

☆

☆

☆

☆ 1

APPALLING

READING LOG

VOLUME **DATE** RATING ☆☆☆☆☆

FORMAT ◯ Physical ◯ Digital **OWNERSHIP** ◯ Owned ◯ Borrowed from: ◯ Other:
NOTES

VOLUME **DATE** RATING ☆☆☆☆☆

FORMAT ◯ Physical ◯ Digital **OWNERSHIP** ◯ Owned ◯ Borrowed from: ◯ Other:
NOTES

VOLUME **DATE** RATING ☆☆☆☆☆

FORMAT ◯ Physical ◯ Digital **OWNERSHIP** ◯ Owned ◯ Borrowed from: ◯ Other:
NOTES

VOLUME **DATE** RATING ☆☆☆☆☆

FORMAT ◯ Physical ◯ Digital **OWNERSHIP** ◯ Owned ◯ Borrowed from: ◯ Other:
NOTES

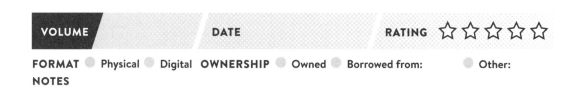

VOLUME **DATE** RATING ☆☆☆☆☆

FORMAT ◯ Physical ◯ Digital **OWNERSHIP** ◯ Owned ◯ Borrowed from: ◯ Other:
NOTES

VOLUME **DATE** RATING ☆☆☆☆☆

FORMAT ◯ Physical ◯ Digital **OWNERSHIP** ◯ Owned ◯ Borrowed from: ◯ Other:
NOTES

READING LOG

VOLUME   **DATE**   **RATING** ☆☆☆☆☆

FORMAT ○ Physical ○ Digital **OWNERSHIP** ○ Owned ○ Borrowed from: ○ Other:
NOTES

VOLUME   **DATE**   **RATING** ☆☆☆☆☆

FORMAT ○ Physical ○ Digital **OWNERSHIP** ○ Owned ○ Borrowed from: ○ Other:
NOTES

VOLUME   **DATE**   **RATING** ☆☆☆☆☆

FORMAT ○ Physical ○ Digital **OWNERSHIP** ○ Owned ○ Borrowed from: ○ Other:
NOTES

VOLUME   **DATE**   **RATING** ☆☆☆☆☆

FORMAT ○ Physical ○ Digital **OWNERSHIP** ○ Owned ○ Borrowed from: ○ Other:
NOTES

VOLUME   **DATE**   **RATING** ☆☆☆☆☆

FORMAT ○ Physical ○ Digital **OWNERSHIP** ○ Owned ○ Borrowed from: ○ Other:
NOTES

VOLUME   **DATE**   **RATING** ☆☆☆☆☆

FORMAT ○ Physical ○ Digital **OWNERSHIP** ○ Owned ○ Borrowed from: ○ Other:
NOTES

VOLUME **DATE** **RATING** ☆☆☆☆☆

FORMAT ● Physical ● Digital **OWNERSHIP** ● Owned ● Borrowed from: ● Other:

NOTES

VOLUME **DATE** **RATING** ☆☆☆☆☆

FORMAT ● Physical ● Digital **OWNERSHIP** ● Owned ● Borrowed from: ● Other:

NOTES

VOLUME **DATE** **RATING** ☆☆☆☆☆

FORMAT ● Physical ● Digital **OWNERSHIP** ● Owned ● Borrowed from: ● Other:

NOTES

VOLUME **DATE** **RATING** ☆☆☆☆☆

FORMAT ● Physical ● Digital **OWNERSHIP** ● Owned ● Borrowed from: ● Other:

NOTES

VOLUME **DATE** **RATING** ☆☆☆☆☆

FORMAT ● Physical ● Digital **OWNERSHIP** ● Owned ● Borrowed from: ● Other:

NOTES

VOLUME **DATE** **RATING** ☆☆☆☆☆

FORMAT ● Physical ● Digital **OWNERSHIP** ● Owned ● Borrowed from: ● Other:

NOTES

PLOT What hooked you on the plot? What storyline kept/keeps you reading?

What would you have done differently? Where did you want this plot to go?

ART What stood out about the art? How did the art fit the story?

CHARACTERS Who's the most compelling character of the series? The honor of best girl/best boy goes to...

This manga is like (or reminds me of)...

Is there an anime adaptation or film for this manga? If not, do you think there should be one?

Additional notes

📖 MANGA SERIES TRACKER

MANGA TITLE

AUTHOR/MANGAKA

First Volume Publication Date

Final Volume Publication Date

GENRE　　○ Shōnen　　○ Shōjo　　○ Seinen　　○ Josei　　○ Kodomomuke (Children's)

INTEREST(S)

- ○ Action-Adventure
- ○ Comedy
- ○ Drama
- ○ Dystopian
- ○ Family
- ○ Fantasy
- ○ History
- ○ Horror

- ○ Isekai
- ○ LGBTQ+
- ○ Martial Arts
- ○ Mecha
- ○ Music
- ○ Mystery/Thriller
- ○ Parody
- ○ Romance

- ○ School Life
- ○ Sci-Fi
- ○ Slice-of-Life
- ○ Sports
- ○ Supernatural
- ○ Superpower
- ○ Other:

PUBLISHER

SERIES STATUS

- ○ Ongoing
- ○ Complete
- ○ Incomplete

TOTAL VOLUMES IN SERIES

MY STATUS

- ○ Plan to Read
- ○ Started Reading
- ○ Completed
- ○ Dropped

SERIES RATING

AMAZING

☆ ⑤

☆

☆

☆

☆ ①

APPALLING

READING LOG

VOLUME　　　　**DATE**　　　　**RATING** ☆☆☆☆☆

FORMAT ● Physical ● Digital **OWNERSHIP** ● Owned ● Borrowed from: ● Other:
NOTES

VOLUME　　　　**DATE**　　　　**RATING** ☆☆☆☆☆

FORMAT ● Physical ● Digital **OWNERSHIP** ● Owned ● Borrowed from: ● Other:
NOTES

VOLUME　　　　**DATE**　　　　**RATING** ☆☆☆☆☆

FORMAT ● Physical ● Digital **OWNERSHIP** ● Owned ● Borrowed from: ● Other:
NOTES

VOLUME　　　　**DATE**　　　　**RATING** ☆☆☆☆☆

FORMAT ● Physical ● Digital **OWNERSHIP** ● Owned ● Borrowed from: ● Other:
NOTES

VOLUME　　　　**DATE**　　　　**RATING** ☆☆☆☆☆

FORMAT ● Physical ● Digital **OWNERSHIP** ● Owned ● Borrowed from: ● Other:
NOTES

VOLUME　　　　**DATE**　　　　**RATING** ☆☆☆☆☆

FORMAT ● Physical ● Digital **OWNERSHIP** ● Owned ● Borrowed from: ● Other:
NOTES

READING LOG

VOLUME   **DATE**   **RATING** ☆☆☆☆☆

FORMAT ⬤ Physical ⬤ Digital   **OWNERSHIP** ⬤ Owned ⬤ Borrowed from: ⬤ Other:

NOTES

VOLUME   **DATE**   **RATING** ☆☆☆☆☆

FORMAT ⬤ Physical ⬤ Digital   **OWNERSHIP** ⬤ Owned ⬤ Borrowed from: ⬤ Other:

NOTES

VOLUME   **DATE**   **RATING** ☆☆☆☆☆

FORMAT ⬤ Physical ⬤ Digital   **OWNERSHIP** ⬤ Owned ⬤ Borrowed from: ⬤ Other:

NOTES

VOLUME   **DATE**   **RATING** ☆☆☆☆☆

FORMAT ⬤ Physical ⬤ Digital   **OWNERSHIP** ⬤ Owned ⬤ Borrowed from: ⬤ Other:

NOTES

VOLUME   **DATE**   **RATING** ☆☆☆☆☆

FORMAT ⬤ Physical ⬤ Digital   **OWNERSHIP** ⬤ Owned ⬤ Borrowed from: ⬤ Other:

NOTES

VOLUME   **DATE**   **RATING** ☆☆☆☆☆

FORMAT ⬤ Physical ⬤ Digital   **OWNERSHIP** ⬤ Owned ⬤ Borrowed from: ⬤ Other:

NOTES

VOLUME **DATE** **RATING** ☆☆☆☆☆

FORMAT ● Physical ● Digital **OWNERSHIP** ● Owned ● Borrowed from: ● Other:

NOTES

VOLUME **DATE** **RATING** ☆☆☆☆☆

FORMAT ● Physical ● Digital **OWNERSHIP** ● Owned ● Borrowed from: ● Other:

NOTES

VOLUME **DATE** **RATING** ☆☆☆☆☆

FORMAT ● Physical ● Digital **OWNERSHIP** ● Owned ● Borrowed from: ● Other:

NOTES

VOLUME **DATE** **RATING** ☆☆☆☆☆

FORMAT ● Physical ● Digital **OWNERSHIP** ● Owned ● Borrowed from: ● Other:

NOTES

VOLUME **DATE** **RATING** ☆☆☆☆☆

FORMAT ● Physical ● Digital **OWNERSHIP** ● Owned ● Borrowed from: ● Other:

NOTES

VOLUME **DATE** **RATING** ☆☆☆☆☆

FORMAT ● Physical ● Digital **OWNERSHIP** ● Owned ● Borrowed from: ● Other:

NOTES

PLOT What hooked you on the plot? What storyline kept/keeps you reading?

What would you have done differently? Where did you want this plot to go?

ART What stood out about the art? How did the art fit the story?

CHARACTERS Who's the most compelling character of the series? The honor of best girl/best boy goes to...

This manga is like (or reminds me of)...

Is there an anime adaptation or film for this manga? If not, do you think there should be one?

Additional notes

📖 MANGA SERIES TRACKER

MANGA TITLE

AUTHOR/MANGAKA

First Volume Publication Date   *Final Volume Publication Date*

GENRE   ○ Shōnen   ○ Shōjo   ○ Seinen   ○ Josei   ○ Kodomomuke (Children's)

INTEREST(S)

○ Action-Adventure   ○ Isekai   ○ School Life
○ Comedy   ○ LGBTQ+   ○ Sci-Fi
○ Drama   ○ Martial Arts   ○ Slice-of-Life
○ Dystopian   ○ Mecha   ○ Sports
○ Family   ○ Music   ○ Supernatural
○ Fantasy   ○ Mystery/Thriller ○ Superpower
○ History   ○ Parody   ○ Other:
○ Horror   ○ Romance

PUBLISHER

SERIES STATUS
○ Ongoing   ○ Complete   ○ Incomplete

TOTAL VOLUMES IN SERIES

MY STATUS   ○ Plan to Read   ○ Completed
                ○ Started Reading   ○ Dropped

SERIES RATING

AMAZING
☆ 5
☆
☆
☆
☆ 1
APPALLING

READING LOG

VOLUME   **DATE**   **RATING** ☆☆☆☆☆

FORMAT ○ Physical ○ Digital   **OWNERSHIP** ○ Owned ○ Borrowed from: ○ Other:

NOTES

VOLUME   **DATE**   **RATING** ☆☆☆☆☆

FORMAT ○ Physical ○ Digital   **OWNERSHIP** ○ Owned ○ Borrowed from: ○ Other:

NOTES

VOLUME   **DATE**   **RATING** ☆☆☆☆☆

FORMAT ○ Physical ○ Digital   **OWNERSHIP** ○ Owned ○ Borrowed from: ○ Other:

NOTES

VOLUME   **DATE**   **RATING** ☆☆☆☆☆

FORMAT ○ Physical ○ Digital   **OWNERSHIP** ○ Owned ○ Borrowed from: ○ Other:

NOTES

VOLUME   **DATE**   **RATING** ☆☆☆☆☆

FORMAT ○ Physical ○ Digital   **OWNERSHIP** ○ Owned ○ Borrowed from: ○ Other:

NOTES

VOLUME   **DATE**   **RATING** ☆☆☆☆☆

FORMAT ○ Physical ○ Digital   **OWNERSHIP** ○ Owned ○ Borrowed from: ○ Other:

NOTES

READING LOG

VOLUME   **DATE**   **RATING** ☆☆☆☆☆

FORMAT ○ Physical ○ Digital   **OWNERSHIP** ○ Owned ○ Borrowed from: ○ Other:

NOTES

VOLUME   **DATE**   **RATING** ☆☆☆☆☆

FORMAT ○ Physical ○ Digital   **OWNERSHIP** ○ Owned ○ Borrowed from: ○ Other:

NOTES

VOLUME   **DATE**   **RATING** ☆☆☆☆☆

FORMAT ○ Physical ○ Digital   **OWNERSHIP** ○ Owned ○ Borrowed from: ○ Other:

NOTES

VOLUME   **DATE**   **RATING** ☆☆☆☆☆

FORMAT ○ Physical ○ Digital   **OWNERSHIP** ○ Owned ○ Borrowed from: ○ Other:

NOTES

VOLUME   **DATE**   **RATING** ☆☆☆☆☆

FORMAT ○ Physical ○ Digital   **OWNERSHIP** ○ Owned ○ Borrowed from: ○ Other:

NOTES

VOLUME   **DATE**   **RATING** ☆☆☆☆☆

FORMAT ○ Physical ○ Digital   **OWNERSHIP** ○ Owned ○ Borrowed from: ○ Other:

NOTES

VOLUME　　　　　　　　　**DATE**　　　　　　　**RATING** ☆ ☆ ☆ ☆ ☆

FORMAT ● Physical ● Digital **OWNERSHIP** ● Owned ● Borrowed from:　　　 ● Other:

NOTES

VOLUME　　　　　　　　　**DATE**　　　　　　　**RATING** ☆ ☆ ☆ ☆ ☆

FORMAT ● Physical ● Digital **OWNERSHIP** ● Owned ● Borrowed from:　　　 ● Other:

NOTES

VOLUME　　　　　　　　　**DATE**　　　　　　　**RATING** ☆ ☆ ☆ ☆ ☆

FORMAT ● Physical ● Digital **OWNERSHIP** ● Owned ● Borrowed from:　　　 ● Other:

NOTES

VOLUME　　　　　　　　　**DATE**　　　　　　　**RATING** ☆ ☆ ☆ ☆ ☆

FORMAT ● Physical ● Digital **OWNERSHIP** ● Owned ● Borrowed from:　　　 ● Other:

NOTES

VOLUME　　　　　　　　　**DATE**　　　　　　　**RATING** ☆ ☆ ☆ ☆ ☆

FORMAT ● Physical ● Digital **OWNERSHIP** ● Owned ● Borrowed from:　　　 ● Other:

NOTES

VOLUME　　　　　　　　　**DATE**　　　　　　　**RATING** ☆ ☆ ☆ ☆ ☆

FORMAT ● Physical ● Digital **OWNERSHIP** ● Owned ● Borrowed from:　　　 ● Other:

NOTES

PLOT What hooked you on the plot? What storyline kept/keeps you reading?

What would you have done differently? Where did you want this plot to go?

ART What stood out about the art? How did the art fit the story?

CHARACTERS Who's the most compelling character of the series? The honor of best girl/best boy goes to...

This manga is like (or reminds me of)...

Is there an anime adaptation or film for this manga? If not, do you think there should be one?

Additional notes

MANGA SERIES TRACKER

MANGA TITLE

AUTHOR/MANGAKA

First Volume Publication Date

Final Volume Publication Date

GENRE ○ Shōnen ○ Shōjo ○ Seinen ○ Josei ○ Kodomomuke (Children's)

INTEREST(S)

- ○ Action-Adventure
- ○ Comedy
- ○ Drama
- ○ Dystopian
- ○ Family
- ○ Fantasy
- ○ History
- ○ Horror

- ○ Isekai
- ○ LGBTQ+
- ○ Martial Arts
- ○ Mecha
- ○ Music
- ○ Mystery/Thriller
- ○ Parody
- ○ Romance

- ○ School Life
- ○ Sci-Fi
- ○ Slice-of-Life
- ○ Sports
- ○ Supernatural
- ○ Superpower
- ○ Other:

PUBLISHER

SERIES STATUS

- ○ Ongoing
- ○ Complete
- ○ Incomplete

TOTAL VOLUMES IN SERIES

MY STATUS

- ○ Plan to Read
- ○ Started Reading
- ○ Completed
- ○ Dropped

SERIES RATING

AMAZING

☆ 5
☆
☆
☆
☆ 1

APPALLING

READING LOG

VOLUME **DATE** **RATING** ☆☆☆☆☆

FORMAT ● Physical ● Digital **OWNERSHIP** ● Owned ● Borrowed from: ● Other:

NOTES

VOLUME **DATE** **RATING** ☆☆☆☆☆

FORMAT ● Physical ● Digital **OWNERSHIP** ● Owned ● Borrowed from: ● Other:

NOTES

VOLUME **DATE** **RATING** ☆☆☆☆☆

FORMAT ● Physical ● Digital **OWNERSHIP** ● Owned ● Borrowed from: ● Other:

NOTES

VOLUME **DATE** **RATING** ☆☆☆☆☆

FORMAT ● Physical ● Digital **OWNERSHIP** ● Owned ● Borrowed from: ● Other:

NOTES

VOLUME **DATE** **RATING** ☆☆☆☆☆

FORMAT ● Physical ● Digital **OWNERSHIP** ● Owned ● Borrowed from: ● Other:

NOTES

VOLUME **DATE** **RATING** ☆☆☆☆☆

FORMAT ● Physical ● Digital **OWNERSHIP** ● Owned ● Borrowed from: ● Other:

NOTES

READING LOG

VOLUME   **DATE**   **RATING** ☆☆☆☆☆

FORMAT ● Physical ● Digital   **OWNERSHIP** ● Owned ● Borrowed from: ● Other:

NOTES

VOLUME   **DATE**   **RATING** ☆☆☆☆☆

FORMAT ● Physical ● Digital   **OWNERSHIP** ● Owned ● Borrowed from: ● Other:

NOTES

VOLUME   **DATE**   **RATING** ☆☆☆☆☆

FORMAT ● Physical ● Digital   **OWNERSHIP** ● Owned ● Borrowed from: ● Other:

NOTES

VOLUME   **DATE**   **RATING** ☆☆☆☆☆

FORMAT ● Physical ● Digital   **OWNERSHIP** ● Owned ● Borrowed from: ● Other:

NOTES

VOLUME   **DATE**   **RATING** ☆☆☆☆☆

FORMAT ● Physical ● Digital   **OWNERSHIP** ● Owned ● Borrowed from: ● Other:

NOTES

VOLUME   **DATE**   **RATING** ☆☆☆☆☆

FORMAT ● Physical ● Digital   **OWNERSHIP** ● Owned ● Borrowed from: ● Other:

NOTES

VOLUME **DATE** **RATING** ☆☆☆☆☆

FORMAT ● Physical ● Digital **OWNERSHIP** ● Owned ● Borrowed from: ● Other:

NOTES

VOLUME **DATE** **RATING** ☆☆☆☆☆

FORMAT ● Physical ● Digital **OWNERSHIP** ● Owned ● Borrowed from: ● Other:

NOTES

VOLUME **DATE** **RATING** ☆☆☆☆☆

FORMAT ● Physical ● Digital **OWNERSHIP** ● Owned ● Borrowed from: ● Other:

NOTES

VOLUME **DATE** **RATING** ☆☆☆☆☆

FORMAT ● Physical ● Digital **OWNERSHIP** ● Owned ● Borrowed from: ● Other:

NOTES

VOLUME **DATE** **RATING** ☆☆☆☆☆

FORMAT ● Physical ● Digital **OWNERSHIP** ● Owned ● Borrowed from: ● Other:

NOTES

VOLUME **DATE** **RATING** ☆☆☆☆☆

FORMAT ● Physical ● Digital **OWNERSHIP** ● Owned ● Borrowed from: ● Other:

NOTES

PLOT What hooked you on the plot? What storyline kept/keeps you reading?

What would you have done differently? Where did you want this plot to go?

ART What stood out about the art? How did the art fit the story?

CHARACTERS Who's the most compelling character of the series? The honor of best girl/best boy goes to...

This manga is like (or reminds me of)...

Is there an anime adaptation or film for this manga? If not, do you think there should be one?

Additional notes

MANGA SERIES TRACKER

MANGA TITLE

AUTHOR/MANGAKA

First Volume Publication Date   *Final Volume Publication Date*

GENRE ○ Shōnen ○ Shōjo ○ Seinen ○ Josei ○ Kodomomuke (Children's)

INTEREST(S)

○ Action-Adventure   ○ Isekai   ○ School Life
○ Comedy   ○ LGBTQ+   ○ Sci-Fi
○ Drama   ○ Martial Arts   ○ Slice-of-Life
○ Dystopian   ○ Mecha   ○ Sports
○ Family   ○ Music   ○ Supernatural
○ Fantasy   ○ Mystery/Thriller   ○ Superpower
○ History   ○ Parody   ○ Other:
○ Horror   ○ Romance

PUBLISHER

SERIES STATUS

○ Ongoing   ○ Complete   ○ Incomplete

TOTAL VOLUMES IN SERIES

MY STATUS   ○ Plan to Read   ○ Completed
                  ○ Started Reading   ○ Dropped

SERIES RATING

AMAZING
☆ 5
☆
☆
☆
☆ 1
APPALLING

READING LOG

VOLUME   **DATE**   **RATING** ☆☆☆☆☆

FORMAT ⬤ Physical ⬤ Digital   **OWNERSHIP** ⬤ Owned ⬤ Borrowed from: ⬤ Other:

NOTES

VOLUME   **DATE**   **RATING** ☆☆☆☆☆

FORMAT ⬤ Physical ⬤ Digital   **OWNERSHIP** ⬤ Owned ⬤ Borrowed from: ⬤ Other:

NOTES

VOLUME   **DATE**   **RATING** ☆☆☆☆☆

FORMAT ⬤ Physical ⬤ Digital   **OWNERSHIP** ⬤ Owned ⬤ Borrowed from: ⬤ Other:

NOTES

VOLUME   **DATE**   **RATING** ☆☆☆☆☆

FORMAT ⬤ Physical ⬤ Digital   **OWNERSHIP** ⬤ Owned ⬤ Borrowed from: ⬤ Other:

NOTES

VOLUME   **DATE**   **RATING** ☆☆☆☆☆

FORMAT ⬤ Physical ⬤ Digital   **OWNERSHIP** ⬤ Owned ⬤ Borrowed from: ⬤ Other:

NOTES

VOLUME   **DATE**   **RATING** ☆☆☆☆☆

FORMAT ⬤ Physical ⬤ Digital   **OWNERSHIP** ⬤ Owned ⬤ Borrowed from: ⬤ Other:

NOTES

READING LOG

VOLUME **DATE** **RATING** ☆☆☆☆☆

FORMAT ● Physical ● Digital **OWNERSHIP** ● Owned ● Borrowed from: ● Other:
NOTES

VOLUME **DATE** **RATING** ☆☆☆☆☆

FORMAT ● Physical ● Digital **OWNERSHIP** ● Owned ● Borrowed from: ● Other:
NOTES

VOLUME **DATE** **RATING** ☆☆☆☆☆

FORMAT ● Physical ● Digital **OWNERSHIP** ● Owned ● Borrowed from: ● Other:
NOTES

VOLUME **DATE** **RATING** ☆☆☆☆☆

FORMAT ● Physical ● Digital **OWNERSHIP** ● Owned ● Borrowed from: ● Other:
NOTES

VOLUME **DATE** **RATING** ☆☆☆☆☆

FORMAT ● Physical ● Digital **OWNERSHIP** ● Owned ● Borrowed from: ● Other:
NOTES

VOLUME **DATE** **RATING** ☆☆☆☆☆

FORMAT ● Physical ● Digital **OWNERSHIP** ● Owned ● Borrowed from: ● Other:
NOTES

VOLUME   **DATE**   **RATING** ⭐☆☆☆☆

FORMAT ⚪ Physical ⚪ Digital **OWNERSHIP** ⚪ Owned ⚪ Borrowed from: ⚪ Other:
NOTES

VOLUME   **DATE**   **RATING** ☆☆☆☆☆

FORMAT ⚪ Physical ⚪ Digital **OWNERSHIP** ⚪ Owned ⚪ Borrowed from: ⚪ Other:
NOTES

VOLUME   **DATE**   **RATING** ☆☆☆☆☆

FORMAT ⚪ Physical ⚪ Digital **OWNERSHIP** ⚪ Owned ⚪ Borrowed from: ⚪ Other:
NOTES

VOLUME   **DATE**   **RATING** ☆☆☆☆☆

FORMAT ⚪ Physical ⚪ Digital **OWNERSHIP** ⚪ Owned ⚪ Borrowed from: ⚪ Other:
NOTES

VOLUME   **DATE**   **RATING** ☆☆☆☆☆

FORMAT ⚪ Physical ⚪ Digital **OWNERSHIP** ⚪ Owned ⚪ Borrowed from: ⚪ Other:
NOTES

VOLUME   **DATE**   **RATING** ☆☆☆☆☆

FORMAT ⚪ Physical ⚪ Digital **OWNERSHIP** ⚪ Owned ⚪ Borrowed from: ⚪ Other:
NOTES

PLOT What hooked you on the plot? What storyline kept/keeps you reading?

What would you have done differently? Where did you want this plot to go?

ART What stood out about the art? How did the art fit the story?

CHARACTERS Who's the most compelling character of the series? The honor of best girl/best boy goes to...

This manga is like (or reminds me of)...

Is there an anime adaptation or film for this manga? If not, do you think there should be one?

Additional notes

📖 MANGA SERIES TRACKER

MANGA TITLE

AUTHOR/MANGAKA

First Volume Publication Date   *Final Volume Publication Date*

GENRE   ○ Shōnen   ○ Shōjo   ○ Seinen   ○ Josei   ○ Kodomomuke (Children's)

INTEREST(S)

- ○ Action-Adventure
- ○ Comedy
- ○ Drama
- ○ Dystopian
- ○ Family
- ○ Fantasy
- ○ History
- ○ Horror

- ○ Isekai
- ○ LGBTQ+
- ○ Martial Arts
- ○ Mecha
- ○ Music
- ○ Mystery/Thriller
- ○ Parody
- ○ Romance

- ○ School Life
- ○ Sci-Fi
- ○ Slice-of-Life
- ○ Sports
- ○ Supernatural
- ○ Superpower
- ○ Other:

PUBLISHER

SERIES STATUS

- ○ Ongoing   ○ Complete   ○ Incomplete

TOTAL VOLUMES IN SERIES

MY STATUS
- ○ Plan to Read   ○ Completed
- ○ Started Reading   ○ Dropped

SERIES RATING

AMAZING

☆ 5
☆
☆
☆
☆ 1

APPALLING

READING LOG

VOLUME   **DATE**   **RATING** ☆ ☆ ☆ ☆ ☆

FORMAT ○ Physical ○ Digital   **OWNERSHIP** ○ Owned ○ Borrowed from: ○ Other:

NOTES

VOLUME   **DATE**   **RATING** ☆ ☆ ☆ ☆ ☆

FORMAT ○ Physical ○ Digital   **OWNERSHIP** ○ Owned ○ Borrowed from: ○ Other:

NOTES

VOLUME   **DATE**   **RATING** ☆ ☆ ☆ ☆ ☆

FORMAT ○ Physical ○ Digital   **OWNERSHIP** ○ Owned ○ Borrowed from: ○ Other:

NOTES

VOLUME   **DATE**   **RATING** ☆ ☆ ☆ ☆ ☆

FORMAT ○ Physical ○ Digital   **OWNERSHIP** ○ Owned ○ Borrowed from: ○ Other:

NOTES

VOLUME   **DATE**   **RATING** ☆ ☆ ☆ ☆ ☆

FORMAT ○ Physical ○ Digital   **OWNERSHIP** ○ Owned ○ Borrowed from: ○ Other:

NOTES

VOLUME   **DATE**   **RATING** ☆ ☆ ☆ ☆ ☆

FORMAT ○ Physical ○ Digital   **OWNERSHIP** ○ Owned ○ Borrowed from: ○ Other:

NOTES

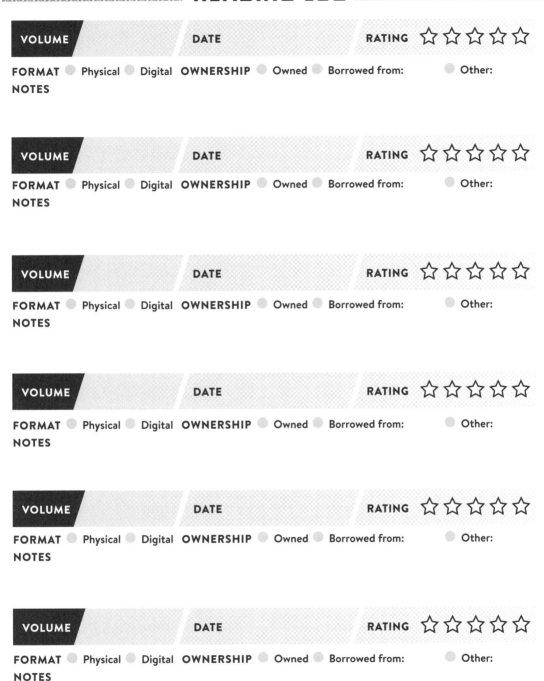

READING LOG

VOLUME **DATE** **RATING** ☆☆☆☆☆

FORMAT ● Physical ● Digital **OWNERSHIP** ● Owned ● Borrowed from: ● Other:

NOTES

VOLUME **DATE** **RATING** ☆☆☆☆☆

FORMAT ● Physical ● Digital **OWNERSHIP** ● Owned ● Borrowed from: ● Other:

NOTES

VOLUME **DATE** **RATING** ☆☆☆☆☆

FORMAT ● Physical ● Digital **OWNERSHIP** ● Owned ● Borrowed from: ● Other:

NOTES

VOLUME **DATE** **RATING** ☆☆☆☆☆

FORMAT ● Physical ● Digital **OWNERSHIP** ● Owned ● Borrowed from: ● Other:

NOTES

VOLUME **DATE** **RATING** ☆☆☆☆☆

FORMAT ● Physical ● Digital **OWNERSHIP** ● Owned ● Borrowed from: ● Other:

NOTES

VOLUME **DATE** **RATING** ☆☆☆☆☆

FORMAT ● Physical ● Digital **OWNERSHIP** ● Owned ● Borrowed from: ● Other:

NOTES

VOLUME   **DATE**   **RATING** ☆☆☆☆☆

FORMAT ○ Physical ○ Digital   **OWNERSHIP** ○ Owned ○ Borrowed from: ○ Other:

NOTES

VOLUME   **DATE**   **RATING** ☆☆☆☆☆

FORMAT ○ Physical ○ Digital   **OWNERSHIP** ○ Owned ○ Borrowed from: ○ Other:

NOTES

VOLUME   **DATE**   **RATING** ☆☆☆☆☆

FORMAT ○ Physical ○ Digital   **OWNERSHIP** ○ Owned ○ Borrowed from: ○ Other:

NOTES

VOLUME   **DATE**   **RATING** ☆☆☆☆☆

FORMAT ○ Physical ○ Digital   **OWNERSHIP** ○ Owned ○ Borrowed from: ○ Other:

NOTES

VOLUME   **DATE**   **RATING** ☆☆☆☆☆

FORMAT ○ Physical ○ Digital   **OWNERSHIP** ○ Owned ○ Borrowed from: ○ Other:

NOTES

VOLUME   **DATE**   **RATING** ☆☆☆☆☆

FORMAT ○ Physical ○ Digital   **OWNERSHIP** ○ Owned ○ Borrowed from: ○ Other:

NOTES

PLOT What hooked you on the plot? What storyline kept/keeps you reading?

What would you have done differently? Where did you want this plot to go?

ART What stood out about the art? How did the art fit the story?

CHARACTERS Who's the most compelling character of the series? The honor of best girl/best boy goes to...

This manga is like (or reminds me of)...

Is there an anime adaptation or film for this manga? If not, do you think there should be one?

Additional notes

📖 MANGA SERIES TRACKER

MANGA TITLE

AUTHOR/MANGAKA

First Volume Publication Date

Final Volume Publication Date

GENRE   ○ Shōnen   ○ Shōjo   ○ Seinen   ○ Josei   ○ Kodomomuke (Children's)

INTEREST(S)

○ Action-Adventure   ○ Isekai   ○ School Life

○ Comedy   ○ LGBTQ+   ○ Sci-Fi

○ Drama   ○ Martial Arts   ○ Slice-of-Life

○ Dystopian   ○ Mecha   ○ Sports

○ Family   ○ Music   ○ Supernatural

○ Fantasy   ○ Mystery/Thriller   ○ Superpower

○ History   ○ Parody   ○ Other:

○ Horror   ○ Romance

PUBLISHER

SERIES STATUS

○ Ongoing   ○ Complete   ○ Incomplete

TOTAL VOLUMES IN SERIES

MY STATUS   ○ Plan to Read   ○ Completed

○ Started Reading   ○ Dropped

SERIES RATING

AMAZING

☆ 5

☆

☆

☆

☆ 1

APPALLING

READING LOG

VOLUME **DATE** **RATING** ☆☆☆☆☆

FORMAT ○ Physical ○ Digital **OWNERSHIP** ○ Owned ○ Borrowed from: ○ Other:
NOTES

VOLUME **DATE** **RATING** ☆☆☆☆☆

FORMAT ○ Physical ○ Digital **OWNERSHIP** ○ Owned ○ Borrowed from: ○ Other:
NOTES

VOLUME **DATE** **RATING** ☆☆☆☆☆

FORMAT ○ Physical ○ Digital **OWNERSHIP** ○ Owned ○ Borrowed from: ○ Other:
NOTES

VOLUME **DATE** **RATING** ☆☆☆☆☆

FORMAT ○ Physical ○ Digital **OWNERSHIP** ○ Owned ○ Borrowed from: ○ Other:
NOTES

VOLUME **DATE** **RATING** ☆☆☆☆☆

FORMAT ○ Physical ○ Digital **OWNERSHIP** ○ Owned ○ Borrowed from: ○ Other:
NOTES

VOLUME **DATE** **RATING** ☆☆☆☆☆

FORMAT ○ Physical ○ Digital **OWNERSHIP** ○ Owned ○ Borrowed from: ○ Other:
NOTES

READING LOG

VOLUME   **DATE**   **RATING** ☆☆☆☆☆

FORMAT ● Physical ● Digital   **OWNERSHIP** ● Owned ● Borrowed from: ● Other:

NOTES

VOLUME   **DATE**   **RATING** ☆☆☆☆☆

FORMAT ● Physical ● Digital   **OWNERSHIP** ● Owned ● Borrowed from: ● Other:

NOTES

VOLUME   **DATE**   **RATING** ☆☆☆☆☆

FORMAT ● Physical ● Digital   **OWNERSHIP** ● Owned ● Borrowed from: ● Other:

NOTES

VOLUME   **DATE**   **RATING** ☆☆☆☆☆

FORMAT ● Physical ● Digital   **OWNERSHIP** ● Owned ● Borrowed from: ● Other:

NOTES

VOLUME   **DATE**   **RATING** ☆☆☆☆☆

FORMAT ● Physical ● Digital   **OWNERSHIP** ● Owned ● Borrowed from: ● Other:

NOTES

VOLUME   **DATE**   **RATING** ☆☆☆☆☆

FORMAT ● Physical ● Digital   **OWNERSHIP** ● Owned ● Borrowed from: ● Other:

NOTES

VOLUME **DATE** **RATING** ☆ ☆ ☆ ☆ ☆

FORMAT Physical Digital **OWNERSHIP** Owned Borrowed from: Other:

NOTES

VOLUME **DATE** **RATING** ☆ ☆ ☆ ☆ ☆

FORMAT Physical Digital **OWNERSHIP** Owned Borrowed from: Other:

NOTES

VOLUME **DATE** **RATING** ☆ ☆ ☆ ☆ ☆

FORMAT Physical Digital **OWNERSHIP** Owned Borrowed from: Other:

NOTES

VOLUME **DATE** **RATING** ☆ ☆ ☆ ☆ ☆

FORMAT Physical Digital **OWNERSHIP** Owned Borrowed from: Other:

NOTES

VOLUME **DATE** **RATING** ☆ ☆ ☆ ☆ ☆

FORMAT Physical Digital **OWNERSHIP** Owned Borrowed from: Other:

NOTES

VOLUME **DATE** **RATING** ☆ ☆ ☆ ☆ ☆

FORMAT Physical Digital **OWNERSHIP** Owned Borrowed from: Other:

NOTES

PLOT What hooked you on the plot? What storyline kept/keeps you reading?

What would you have done differently? Where did you want this plot to go?

ART What stood out about the art? How did the art fit the story?

CHARACTERS Who's the most compelling character of the series? The honor of best girl/best boy goes to...

This manga is like (or reminds me of)...

Is there an anime adaptation or film for this manga? If not, do you think there should be one?

Additional notes

MANGA SERIES TRACKER

MANGA TITLE

AUTHOR/MANGAKA

First Volume Publication Date

Final Volume Publication Date

GENRE ○ Shōnen ○ Shōjo ○ Seinen ○ Josei ○ Kodomomuke (Children's)

INTEREST(S)

- ○ Action-Adventure
- ○ Comedy
- ○ Drama
- ○ Dystopian
- ○ Family
- ○ Fantasy
- ○ History
- ○ Horror

- ○ Isekai
- ○ LGBTQ+
- ○ Martial Arts
- ○ Mecha
- ○ Music
- ○ Mystery/Thriller
- ○ Parody
- ○ Romance

- ○ School Life
- ○ Sci-Fi
- ○ Slice-of-Life
- ○ Sports
- ○ Supernatural
- ○ Superpower
- ○ Other:

PUBLISHER

SERIES STATUS

○ Ongoing ○ Complete ○ Incomplete

TOTAL VOLUMES IN SERIES

MY STATUS
- ○ Plan to Read
- ○ Started Reading
- ○ Completed
- ○ Dropped

SERIES RATING

AMAZING

☆ 5

☆

☆

☆

☆ 1

APPALLING

VOLUME **DATE** **RATING** ☆☆☆☆☆

FORMAT ◯ Physical ◯ Digital **OWNERSHIP** ◯ Owned ◯ Borrowed from: ◯ Other:

NOTES

VOLUME **DATE** **RATING** ☆☆☆☆☆

FORMAT ◯ Physical ◯ Digital **OWNERSHIP** ◯ Owned ◯ Borrowed from: ◯ Other:

NOTES

VOLUME **DATE** **RATING** ☆☆☆☆☆

FORMAT ◯ Physical ◯ Digital **OWNERSHIP** ◯ Owned ◯ Borrowed from: ◯ Other:

NOTES

VOLUME **DATE** **RATING** ☆☆☆☆☆

FORMAT ◯ Physical ◯ Digital **OWNERSHIP** ◯ Owned ◯ Borrowed from: ◯ Other:

NOTES

VOLUME **DATE** **RATING** ☆☆☆☆☆

FORMAT ◯ Physical ◯ Digital **OWNERSHIP** ◯ Owned ◯ Borrowed from: ◯ Other:

NOTES

VOLUME **DATE** **RATING** ☆☆☆☆☆

FORMAT ◯ Physical ◯ Digital **OWNERSHIP** ◯ Owned ◯ Borrowed from: ◯ Other:

NOTES

READING LOG

VOLUME **DATE** **RATING** ☆☆☆☆☆

FORMAT ● Physical ● Digital **OWNERSHIP** ● Owned ● Borrowed from: ● Other:
NOTES

VOLUME **DATE** **RATING** ☆☆☆☆☆

FORMAT ● Physical ● Digital **OWNERSHIP** ● Owned ● Borrowed from: ● Other:
NOTES

VOLUME **DATE** **RATING** ☆☆☆☆☆

FORMAT ● Physical ● Digital **OWNERSHIP** ● Owned ● Borrowed from: ● Other:
NOTES

VOLUME **DATE** **RATING** ☆☆☆☆☆

FORMAT ● Physical ● Digital **OWNERSHIP** ● Owned ● Borrowed from: ● Other:
NOTES

VOLUME **DATE** **RATING** ☆☆☆☆☆

FORMAT ● Physical ● Digital **OWNERSHIP** ● Owned ● Borrowed from: ● Other:
NOTES

VOLUME **DATE** **RATING** ☆☆☆☆☆

FORMAT ● Physical ● Digital **OWNERSHIP** ● Owned ● Borrowed from: ● Other:
NOTES

VOLUME   **DATE**   **RATING** ☆☆☆☆☆

FORMAT ◦ Physical ◦ Digital   **OWNERSHIP** ◦ Owned ◦ Borrowed from: ◦ Other:

NOTES

VOLUME   **DATE**   **RATING** ☆☆☆☆☆

FORMAT ◦ Physical ◦ Digital   **OWNERSHIP** ◦ Owned ◦ Borrowed from: ◦ Other:

NOTES

VOLUME   **DATE**   **RATING** ☆☆☆☆☆

FORMAT ◦ Physical ◦ Digital   **OWNERSHIP** ◦ Owned ◦ Borrowed from: ◦ Other:

NOTES

VOLUME   **DATE**   **RATING** ☆☆☆☆☆

FORMAT ◦ Physical ◦ Digital   **OWNERSHIP** ◦ Owned ◦ Borrowed from: ◦ Other:

NOTES

VOLUME   **DATE**   **RATING** ☆☆☆☆☆

FORMAT ◦ Physical ◦ Digital   **OWNERSHIP** ◦ Owned ◦ Borrowed from: ◦ Other:

NOTES

VOLUME   **DATE**   **RATING** ☆☆☆☆☆

FORMAT ◦ Physical ◦ Digital   **OWNERSHIP** ◦ Owned ◦ Borrowed from: ◦ Other:

NOTES

PLOT What hooked you on the plot? What storyline kept/keeps you reading?

What would you have done differently? Where did you want this plot to go?

ART What stood out about the art? How did the art fit the story?

CHARACTERS Who's the most compelling character of the series? The honor of best girl/best boy goes to...

This manga is like (or reminds me of)...

Is there an anime adaptation or film for this manga? If not, do you think there should be one?

Additional notes

MANGA TITLE

AUTHOR/MANGAKA

First Volume Publication Date

Final Volume Publication Date

GENRE　　○ Shōnen　　○ Shōjo　　○ Seinen　　○ Josei　　○ Kodomomuke (Children's)

INTEREST(S)

- Action-Adventure
- Comedy
- Drama
- Dystopian
- Family
- Fantasy
- History
- Horror

- Isekai
- LGBTQ+
- Martial Arts
- Mecha
- Music
- Mystery/Thriller
- Parody
- Romance

- School Life
- Sci-Fi
- Slice-of-Life
- Sports
- Supernatural
- Superpower
- Other:

PUBLISHER

SERIES STATUS
- Ongoing
- Complete
- Incomplete

TOTAL VOLUMES IN SERIES

MY STATUS
- Plan to Read
- Started Reading
- Completed
- Dropped

SERIES RATING

AMAZING

☆ 5
☆
☆
☆
☆ 1

APPALLING

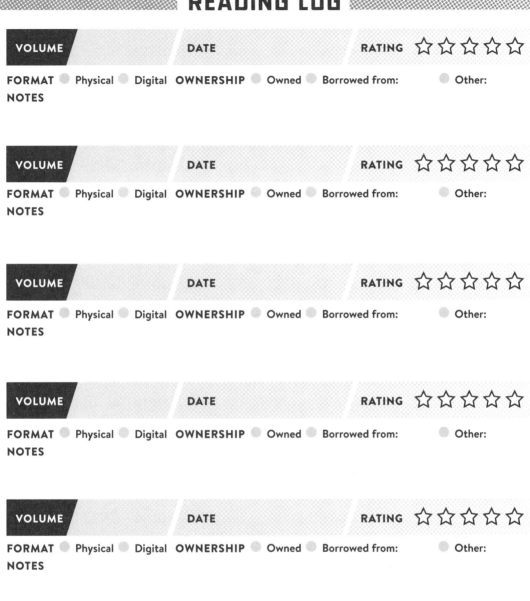

VOLUME **DATE** **RATING** ☆☆☆☆☆
FORMAT ○ Physical ○ Digital **OWNERSHIP** ○ Owned ○ Borrowed from: ○ Other:
NOTES

VOLUME **DATE** **RATING** ☆☆☆☆☆
FORMAT ○ Physical ○ Digital **OWNERSHIP** ○ Owned ○ Borrowed from: ○ Other:
NOTES

VOLUME **DATE** **RATING** ☆☆☆☆☆
FORMAT ○ Physical ○ Digital **OWNERSHIP** ○ Owned ○ Borrowed from: ○ Other:
NOTES

VOLUME **DATE** **RATING** ☆☆☆☆☆
FORMAT ○ Physical ○ Digital **OWNERSHIP** ○ Owned ○ Borrowed from: ○ Other:
NOTES

VOLUME **DATE** **RATING** ☆☆☆☆☆
FORMAT ○ Physical ○ Digital **OWNERSHIP** ○ Owned ○ Borrowed from: ○ Other:
NOTES

VOLUME **DATE** **RATING** ☆☆☆☆☆
FORMAT ○ Physical ○ Digital **OWNERSHIP** ○ Owned ○ Borrowed from: ○ Other:
NOTES

READING LOG

VOLUME **DATE** **RATING** ☆☆☆☆☆

FORMAT ● Physical ● Digital **OWNERSHIP** ● Owned ● Borrowed from: ● Other:
NOTES

VOLUME **DATE** **RATING** ☆☆☆☆☆

FORMAT ● Physical ● Digital **OWNERSHIP** ● Owned ● Borrowed from: ● Other:
NOTES

VOLUME **DATE** **RATING** ☆☆☆☆☆

FORMAT ● Physical ● Digital **OWNERSHIP** ● Owned ● Borrowed from: ● Other:
NOTES

VOLUME **DATE** **RATING** ☆☆☆☆☆

FORMAT ● Physical ● Digital **OWNERSHIP** ● Owned ● Borrowed from: ● Other:
NOTES

VOLUME **DATE** **RATING** ☆☆☆☆☆

FORMAT ● Physical ● Digital **OWNERSHIP** ● Owned ● Borrowed from: ● Other:
NOTES

VOLUME **DATE** **RATING** ☆☆☆☆☆

FORMAT ● Physical ● Digital **OWNERSHIP** ● Owned ● Borrowed from: ● Other:
NOTES

VOLUME **DATE** RATING ☆☆☆☆☆

FORMAT ○ Physical ○ Digital **OWNERSHIP** ○ Owned ○ Borrowed from: ○ Other:
NOTES

VOLUME **DATE** RATING ☆☆☆☆☆

FORMAT ○ Physical ○ Digital **OWNERSHIP** ○ Owned ○ Borrowed from: ○ Other:
NOTES

VOLUME **DATE** RATING ☆☆☆☆☆

FORMAT ○ Physical ○ Digital **OWNERSHIP** ○ Owned ○ Borrowed from: ○ Other:
NOTES

VOLUME **DATE** RATING ☆☆☆☆☆

FORMAT ○ Physical ○ Digital **OWNERSHIP** ○ Owned ○ Borrowed from: ○ Other:
NOTES

VOLUME **DATE** RATING ☆☆☆☆☆

FORMAT ○ Physical ○ Digital **OWNERSHIP** ○ Owned ○ Borrowed from: ○ Other:
NOTES

VOLUME **DATE** RATING ☆☆☆☆☆

FORMAT ○ Physical ○ Digital **OWNERSHIP** ○ Owned ○ Borrowed from: ○ Other:
NOTES

MY SERIES NOTES

PLOT What hooked you on the plot? What storyline kept/keeps you reading?

What would you have done differently? Where did you want this plot to go?

ART What stood out about the art? How did the art fit the story?

CHARACTERS Who's the most compelling character of the series? The honor of best girl/best boy goes to...

This manga is like (or reminds me of)...

Is there an anime adaptation or film for this manga? If not, do you think there should be one?

Additional notes

MANGA SERIES TRACKER

MANGA TITLE

AUTHOR/MANGAKA

First Volume Publication Date

Final Volume Publication Date

GENRE
- Shōnen
- Shōjo
- Seinen
- Josei
- Kodomomuke (Children's)

INTEREST(S)
- Action-Adventure
- Comedy
- Drama
- Dystopian
- Family
- Fantasy
- History
- Horror
- Isekai
- LGBTQ+
- Martial Arts
- Mecha
- Music
- Mystery/Thriller
- Parody
- Romance
- School Life
- Sci-Fi
- Slice-of-Life
- Sports
- Supernatural
- Superpower
- Other:

PUBLISHER

SERIES STATUS
- Ongoing
- Complete
- Incomplete

TOTAL VOLUMES IN SERIES

MY STATUS
- Plan to Read
- Started Reading
- Completed
- Dropped

SERIES RATING

AMAZING
- ☆ 5
- ☆
- ☆
- ☆
- ☆ 1

APPALLING

READING LOG

VOLUME　　　　　　**DATE**　　　　　　**RATING** ☆☆☆☆☆

FORMAT ● Physical ● Digital **OWNERSHIP** ● Owned ● Borrowed from: ● Other:
NOTES

VOLUME　　　　　　**DATE**　　　　　　**RATING** ☆☆☆☆☆

FORMAT ● Physical ● Digital **OWNERSHIP** ● Owned ● Borrowed from: ● Other:
NOTES

VOLUME　　　　　　**DATE**　　　　　　**RATING** ☆☆☆☆☆

FORMAT ● Physical ● Digital **OWNERSHIP** ● Owned ● Borrowed from: ● Other:
NOTES

VOLUME　　　　　　**DATE**　　　　　　**RATING** ☆☆☆☆☆

FORMAT ● Physical ● Digital **OWNERSHIP** ● Owned ● Borrowed from: ● Other:
NOTES

VOLUME　　　　　　**DATE**　　　　　　**RATING** ☆☆☆☆☆

FORMAT ● Physical ● Digital **OWNERSHIP** ● Owned ● Borrowed from: ● Other:
NOTES

VOLUME　　　　　　**DATE**　　　　　　**RATING** ☆☆☆☆☆

FORMAT ● Physical ● Digital **OWNERSHIP** ● Owned ● Borrowed from: ● Other:
NOTES

READING LOG

VOLUME **DATE** **RATING** ☆☆☆☆☆

FORMAT ○ Physical ○ Digital **OWNERSHIP** ○ Owned ○ Borrowed from: ○ Other:
NOTES

VOLUME **DATE** **RATING** ☆☆☆☆☆

FORMAT ○ Physical ○ Digital **OWNERSHIP** ○ Owned ○ Borrowed from: ○ Other:
NOTES

VOLUME **DATE** **RATING** ☆☆☆☆☆

FORMAT ○ Physical ○ Digital **OWNERSHIP** ○ Owned ○ Borrowed from: ○ Other:
NOTES

VOLUME **DATE** **RATING** ☆☆☆☆☆

FORMAT ○ Physical ○ Digital **OWNERSHIP** ○ Owned ○ Borrowed from: ○ Other:
NOTES

VOLUME **DATE** **RATING** ☆☆☆☆☆

FORMAT ○ Physical ○ Digital **OWNERSHIP** ○ Owned ○ Borrowed from: ○ Other:
NOTES

VOLUME **DATE** **RATING** ☆☆☆☆☆

FORMAT ○ Physical ○ Digital **OWNERSHIP** ○ Owned ○ Borrowed from: ○ Other:
NOTES

VOLUME **DATE** **RATING** ☆☆☆☆☆

FORMAT ● Physical ● Digital **OWNERSHIP** ● Owned ● Borrowed from: ● Other:

NOTES

VOLUME **DATE** **RATING** ☆☆☆☆☆

FORMAT ● Physical ● Digital **OWNERSHIP** ● Owned ● Borrowed from: ● Other:

NOTES

VOLUME **DATE** **RATING** ☆☆☆☆☆

FORMAT ● Physical ● Digital **OWNERSHIP** ● Owned ● Borrowed from: ● Other:

NOTES

VOLUME **DATE** **RATING** ☆☆☆☆☆

FORMAT ● Physical ● Digital **OWNERSHIP** ● Owned ● Borrowed from: ● Other:

NOTES

VOLUME **DATE** **RATING** ☆☆☆☆☆

FORMAT ● Physical ● Digital **OWNERSHIP** ● Owned ● Borrowed from: ● Other:

NOTES

VOLUME **DATE** **RATING** ☆☆☆☆☆

FORMAT ● Physical ● Digital **OWNERSHIP** ● Owned ● Borrowed from: ● Other:

NOTES

PLOT What hooked you on the plot? What storyline kept/keeps you reading?

What would you have done differently? Where did you want this plot to go?

ART What stood out about the art? How did the art fit the story?

CHARACTERS Who's the most compelling character of the series? The honor of best girl/best boy goes to...

This manga is like (or reminds me of)...

Is there an anime adaptation or film for this manga? If not, do you think there should be one?

Additional notes

MY MANGA LISTS

There is so much manga still out there to read! In this My Manga Lists section, you'll get an insider look at my top fifty rankings for all manga, create your own top fifty list (to keep to yourself or to give recommendations to others), and keep a list of your must-buy manga.

TOP 50 LISTS

The top fifty lists give you great suggestions for which manga to buy next and space to log your favorites in ranked order! Vernieda's (my) Top 50 List has titles from different genres and features a variety of storytelling styles, so there's something for everyone. And while there are many recognizable manga series listed here, personal taste is individual and unique, so you may disagree with my choices and their order. That's where your My Top 50 List comes in. Create your take on a top fifty list in these pages.

VERNIEDA'S TOP 50 LIST

1 *Frieren: Beyond Journey's End* by Kanehito Yamada and Tsukasa Abe. VIZ Media.

2 *Clover* by CLAMP. Kodansha.

3 *Fullmetal Alchemist* by Hiromu Arakawa. VIZ Media.

4 *Blade of the Immortal* by Hiroaki Samura. Dark Horse Comics.

5 *Sailor Moon* by Naoko Takeuchi. Kodansha.

6 *Demon Slayer: Kimetsu no Yaiba* by Koyoharu Gotouge. VIZ Media.

7 *My Brother's Husband* by Gengoroh Tagame. Pantheon.

8 *Claymore* by Norihiro Yagi. VIZ Media.

9 *A Bride's Story* by Kaoru Mori. Yen Press.

10 *Spy x Family* by Tatsuya Endo. VIZ Media.

11 *A Sign of Affection* by suu Morishita. Kodansha.

12 *Look Back* by Tatsuki Fujimoto. VIZ Media.

13 *The Rose of Versailles* by Riyoko Ikeda. Udon Entertainment.

14 *A Man and His Cat* by Umi Sakurai. Square Enix Manga.

15 *Boys Run the Riot* by Keito Gaku. Kodansha.

16 *My Love Story!!* by Kazune Kawahara and Aruko. VIZ Media.

17 *Blood on the Tracks* by Shuzo Oshimi. Kodansha.

18 *Uzumaki* by Junji Ito. VIZ Media.

19 *Given* by Natsuki Kizu. SuBLime.

20 *Tokyo Ghoul* by Sui Ishida. VIZ Media.

21 *Lady Snowblood* by Kazuo Koike and Kazuo Kamimura. Dark Horse Comics.

22 *Monster* by Naoki Urasawa. VIZ Media.

23 *Paradise Kiss* by Ai Yazawa. Kodansha.

24 *The Way of the Househusband* by Kousuke Oono. VIZ Media.

25 *Witch Hat Atelier* by Kamome Shirahama. Kodansha.

26 *Jujutsu Kaisen* by Gege Akutami. VIZ Media.

27 *Devilman* by Go Nagai. Seven Seas Entertainment.

28 *Real* by Takehiko Inoue. VIZ Media.

29 *Days on Fes* by Kanato Oka. Yen Press.

30 *Snow White with the Red Hair* by Sorata Akiduki. VIZ Media.

31 *Our Dreams at Dusk* by Yuhki Kamatani. Seven Seas Entertainment.

32 *One-Punch Man* by ONE and Yusuke Murata. VIZ Media.

33 *Black Butler* by Yana Toboso. Yen Press.

34 *Naruto* by Masashi Kishimoto. VIZ Media.

35 *Akira* by Katsuhiro Otomo. Kodansha.

36 *Lupin III: Greatest Heists* by Monkey Punch. Seven Seas Entertainment.

37 *Yotsuba&!* by Kiyohiko Azuma. Yen Press.

38 *Ōoku: The Inner Chambers* by Fumi Yoshinaga. VIZ Media.

39 *Chi's Sweet Home* by Konami Kanata. Vertical Comics.

40 *My Dress-Up Darling* by Shinichi Fukuda. Square Enix Manga.

41 *Descending Stories* by Haruko Kumota. Kodansha.

42 *JoJo's Bizarre Adventure* by Hirohiko Araki. VIZ Media.

43 *Wotakoi: Love Is Hard for Otaku* by Fujita. Kodansha.

44 *Fruits Basket* by Natsuki Takaya. Yen Press.

45 *Princess Jellyfish* by Akiko Higashimura. Kodansha.

46 *Haikyu!!* by Haruichi Furudate. VIZ Media.

47 *Mushishi* by Yuki Urushibara. Kodansha.

48 *Death Note* by Tsugumi Ohba and Takeshi Obata. VIZ Media.

49 *Saint Young Men* by Hikaru Nakamura. Kodansha.

50 *Inuyasha* by Rumiko Takahashi. VIZ Media.

MY TOP 50 LIST

1	13
2	14
3	15
4	16
5	17
6	18
7	19
8	20
9	21
10	22
11	23
12	24

25	38
26	39
27	40
28	41
29	42
30	43
31	44
32	45
33	46
34	47
35	48
36	49
37	50

MY MUST-BUY LIST

There's lots of manga out there, and you need a space to write down what you plan to buy next so you don't forget. Write any volumes/series you want to read here so you remember what you need when you head out to your favorite bookstore or library, or when you get ready to download a new set of volumes.

ABOUT THE AUTHOR

Vernieda Vergara first discovered manga as a teenager when a friend gave her a copy of *Battle Angel Alita* for her birthday. The introduction sparked a lifelong affair with Japanese comics that continues to this day. Vernieda's manga must-read lists, anime reviews, articles, and more have appeared on sites including *Den of Geek*, *Book Riot*, and *Women Write About Comics*. She lives in the suburbs of Washington, DC, where she practices yoga, drinks far too much bubble tea, and takes care of even more houseplants.